THE NISSAN ENIGMA

The Nissan Enigma

Flexibility at Work in a Local Economy

Philip Garrahan and Paul Stewart

MANSELL

First published in 1992 by
Mansell Publishing Limited, *A Cassell Imprint*
Villiers House, 41/47 Strand, London WC2N 5JE, England
387 Park Avenue South, New York, NY 10016-8810, USA

British Library Cataloguing in Publication Data
Garrahan, Philip
   The Nissan enigma: flexibility at work in a local economy.
   1. North-East England. Cars. Production. Industrial relations
   I. Title   II. Stewart, Paul   III. Nissan Jidosha Kabushiki Kaisha
331.04292220942871

ISBN 0-7201-2020-9

Library of Congress Cataloging-in-Publication Data
Garrahan, Philip.
   The Nissan enigma: Flexibility at work in a local economy /
Philip Garrahan and Paul Stewart.
       p.   cm.
   Includes bibliographical references and index.
   ISBN 0-7201-2020-9
   1. Nissan Motor Manufacturing (UK)—Management. 2. Nissan Motor
Manufacturing (UK)—Employees. 3. Automobile industry and trade—
England—Sunderland—Management. 4. Automobile industry workers—
England—Sunderland. I. Stewart. Paul. II. Title.
HD9710.G74N574   1992
338.7'629222'0942871—dc20   91-15255
                                                      CIP

Typeset by Colset Private Limited, Singapore
Printed and bound in Great Britain by
Biddles Ltd, Guildford and King's Lynn

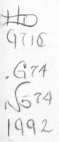

For Judith and Veronica

Contents

Preface

The term 'post-Fordism' has entered contemporary debate about economic, political and social change largely as though it marked the end of an old era and the beginning of something new. In fact, post-Fordism has been used before to refer to a transitionary period of industrial development around the late 1960s and early 1970s. Is there any reason, therefore, why we should accord it more significance now than when it was used almost two decades ago? The answer to this question almost certainly has something to do with current patterns of global capital investment. Twenty years ago post-Fordism denoted an upgrading of automation and mechanisation in manufacturing, and investment from the USA led the way. Today, it is Japanese investment in both the USA and Europe which is primarily associated with new developments in manufacturing. These new developments are as much to do with the organisation of work and production as they are to do with automation, and in this respect there is a difference in the way the term 'post-Fordism' is used.

In this book we are not principally concerned with entering into a debate about the extent of Fordism's global demise. Nevertheless, we are concerned that any analysis based on the assumption that Fordism is on the wane should be capable of telling us how social domination has been transformed. To show the truth, if any, in Fordism's demise, one would have to illustrate how new technologies and methods of production might overcome social subordination (including class domination). Also, there would need to be some explanation of how new management strategies are transforming one of the fundamental features of all management under capitalism—the requirement to ensure the exploitation and subordination of labour—such that class antagonism becomes either impossible or at best, highly unlikely. This, post-Fordists argue, is because the new management and ideological features of flexible production strategies provide employees with real meaning in their lives at work. Fordism is relevant not just to manufacturing industries, but to the whole political economy of social relations in advanced capitalism. The main elements of a Fordist system might be private capital represented by companies, the trade union (or other means for organising workers) and the modern state. And, given that it is more than a description of, let us say, the car industry, the main components of a Fordist social system linked to state intervention sets demanding research questions beyond our intentions here. The problematical issue is that however much of a transition modern economies are experiencing, it is far too soon to determine a single trajectory of development. Thus, the term 'post-Fordism' has a relevant but limited analytical use, falling far short of the requirements for challenging the whole body of empirical and conceptual evidence for Fordism (Allen and Massey, 1988).

At the heart of the argument about contemporary restructuring lies the view that Fordism is more an account of an era in industrial development than it is an explanation for a complete and enduring socio-economic system linked to specific forms of state intervention. Since mass production of cars, among other things, clearly became significant in the interwar and post-1945 years, there exists a quite understandable tendency to see Fordism as relevant to that time in the history of the twentieth century. The Fordist emphasis is upon volume or mass production directed not at sales in the first instance, but at creating markets with demand for constantly increasing output.

The abundant evidence for economic restructuring in the 1980s has led some commentators into an excessive reliance on periodisation: thus, the 1980s are regarded as the dawning of the age of post-Fordism, a 'New Times' in which class conflict is replaced by consumer politics, state intervention in the economy gives way to a process of recommodification, and mass production and mass consumption (the hallmarks of Fordism) give way to flexible systems quickly responsive to fashions and individual preferences. Post-Fordism is about adjusting output to meet consumer demands and thus the emphasis is on production flexibility. A different response to current economic restructuring is the one which we favour: that novel practices are emerging (whether in manufacturing or service industries, the public sector, the finance sector, and so on), but that these hardly constitute a reformulation of the Fordist system and class antagonism. Our purpose in this debate is to make an empirical contribution about corporate control of the local economy: we aim to show that flexibility within Nissan and the company's emphasis on teamworking and quality form the context for a system of extended social control and surveillance of the workforce.

We are concerned with the extent to which new management practices are emerging which could be said to transcend the imperative of social control (in terms of class) which is writ large in the organisational culture of Fordism. The hallmarks of the new era are supposedly the creation of new management strategies that allow for actual employee control of work and, as a consequence, the displacement of management–employee antagonism (class conflict). It is argued that this is highlighted by the active involvement of employees themselves. This occurs at a level of production held up as an exemplar of the success of this transformation of working life, i.e. worker commitment to and control of the practice of quality. It is no accident that this constitutes the mainstay of the Nissan production system, the 'Nissan Way'. It is only when we carefully unpack the ideological baggage portraying the pursuit of quality as a natural and inevitable given that we perceive not only the conflict it seeks to displace (class) but also another type of conflict (individual peer competition), which it encourages. For the fact is that the company's very ideological notion of quality has to be constructed every day in all the institutions set up to safeguard consent. Consent is truly manufactured, although contrary to Burawoy (1979) we argue that its success is achieved not only at the level of the internal labour process. We are interested then in the elaboration of consensus for quality on the line as a mechanism of social control. This depends upon the daily infusion of an imperative of individual and group competition. If the traditional forms of conflict, supposedly associated with the declining Fordist era, are indeed diminishing we cannot see why at Nissan so much time, money and effort are devoted to making sure they cannot appear in their old guise. An elaborate system of company-sanctioned conflicts (peer competition and intergroup rivalry) is allowed. The sublimated conflict is reflected upon in Chapter 5. In short, the success of the internal factory regime depends upon what we term a 'new regime of subordination' which extends from a local consensus in favour of corporate control of external resources to a careful construction of an internal organisational culture that leaves the unconvinced with few alternatives in an area of high unemployment. This is a far cry from the optimism championed in a post-Fordist future.

In researching this book we have received generous assistance from many quarters. Local public bodies consulted include the North of England Development Council, the Northern Development Company, the Washington Development Corporation, Tyne and Wear County Council, Sunderland Borough Council, the Tyne and Wear Development Corporation, the Trade Union Studies Information Unit, and the Newcastle and Sunderland Centres for the Unemployed. While such bodies and locally elected MPs, MEPs, and councillors have always been willing to discuss with us new inward investment and its effect on the local economy, this book could not have been written without the willing cooperation of Nissan workers. Only one of the twenty workers we contacted refused to be interviewed. Out of preference for conducting in-depth interviews away from the demands and possible interruptions of manufacturing work, we visited Nissan workers at their homes. Since the interviews with each worker typically lasted two hours, we are grateful to them for their time and hospitality, and patience. In acknowledging their assistance, mention must also be made of the respect for confidentiality and the decision we made to refer to them by pseudonyms.

Our research assistant, Carol Stephenson, bore the brunt of arranging interviews and making transcripts of the interviews, and we are grateful to her for this and for her unstinting professional support. Our thanks also go to under-graduate and postgraduate students at Sunderland Polytechnic for joining in the debates in this book, especially undergraduates taking our 'Industry and Organ-isations' and 'Urban and Regional Politics' courses and the MA in Local Social Studies. During the last two years several opportunities arose to discuss some of the arguments in this book with colleagues and friends both in Britain and the USA. We particularly want to thank colleagues at meetings and conferences in Newcastle, Edinburgh, Warwick, Sheffield, Surrey, Ann Arbor and Chicago. Finally we acknowledge the generous financial support of the research committee at Sunderland Polytechnic, as well as the time given us by other colleagues researching in the Local Studies Unit.

Chapter 1: **Cars or People?**

INTRODUCTION: WHY AN ENIGMA

This book is primarily about the people who work in the changing auto industry in Britain. The auto industry is the world's biggest manufacturing industry: it employs more people and uses more raw materials than any other sector of industry. So, when an industrial giant like Nissan sites a major production platform in Britain, it is not only local communities and observers who take notice. Events in Sunderland, the location of Nissan's first greenfield facility in Europe, will have ramifications for everyone working for firms that make motor vehicles. The reason for this is the commercially acknowledged competitive advantage which Japanese companies presently possess, allowing them to produce vehicles more efficiently and thus generate higher profits. The International Motor Vehicle Programme reported on the current assembly time advantage of Japanese auto firms: whereas the assembly of a typical volume-produced car in the European Community took 36 hours, Japanese firms achieve the same in 20 hours or less (NCC, 1990). Existing auto manufacturers in Britain and the rest of Europe (many, but not all, of them with US parent companies) are thus watching the Nissan development with special concern for their own market shares.

Now that Nissan's investment is joined by those of Toyota in Derbyshire and of Honda in Swindon, the full evidence is there of a Japanese commitment to winning an increasing share of European Community vehicle sales during the 1990s. Indeed, by the middle of the decade these three companies will have the capacity for producing half a million vehicles in Britain, equivalent to one-quarter of the existing UK market alone.

Close scrutiny of Nissan and other Japanese car firms is not the sole preserve of company executives planning market strategies, however. Management and workers alike are driven by the same imperative to understand the reasons for the greater productivity in 'the Japanese way' of making and selling cars. Companies respond to market pressures, and with Nissan's success, at least some of its methods will be copied. There will be a substantial impact on the people who work in the auto and related industries, where new working practices and 'Just-In-Time' manufacturing systems are being developed. Thus, it is the new management strategies and innovations in the organisation of work which concern us most, and which are related to the radical changes in Sunderland's local political economy.

Figure 1 Sunderland in the UK.

There is already evidence of widespread adaptation of some aspects of Japanese manufacturing systems, and some authors have described this as a process of 'Japanisation' in British industry (Oliver and Wilkinson, 1988). Our objective is not to speculate on how successful other firms will be in imitating production methods refined in Japan and now being installed in various ways throughout Western economies. Instead, we aim to examine how far Nissan has gone in adapting its blueprint for auto manufacturing to conditions in the North-East of England, and then proceed to assess the effect that this is having on those who work for the company. This important distinction is made at the outset, since our study and its conclusions are primarily about the Nissan development in Sunderland, although no doubt there will be useful parallels to be drawn and comparisons to be made.

Nissan is an enigma because as a promoter of industrial change it is not all that it seems, and because there are some elements of Nissan's public relations image which do not stand up to closer examination. An enigma is something which is at first hard to understand and which, like a puzzle, does not readily lend itself to a straightforward interpretation even though there is one in existence. On the surface, Nissan would seem to be the leading firm with a high-technology status in the Sunderland area, which is characterised by old, inefficient and declining industries. Nissan has gained a professionally publicised reputation for reforging the industrial worker's experience: its best-known spokesperson advertises a company system which utilises participative management approaches, and which humanises industrial work by empowering workers through multi-skilling and team efforts, and by giving them the satisfaction of producing quality goods (Wickens, 1987). Gone, it is alleged, are the rigidities and frictions of multiple job demarcations, and the associated industrial relations turmoil of past British motor vehicle manufacturing. In the place of workers adhering to divided and divisive trade unions, Nissan's boast is that loyalty to the company is the modern way forward to growth and prosperity. And so Nissan is also inextricably tied to the 'new realism' of industrial relations, claiming that there is less need for organised labour in a company which treats its employees as individual members of one large, and contented, family. Whether all of this really is the stuff of a new industrial revolution is at the heart of this book.

The analysis presented in later chapters necessarily draws on several areas of academic interest, principally linking the analysis of local political economy with the sociology of work organisation. Paramount among the ideas contested by our argument is that industrial life previously arranged according to 'Fordist' principles of production is undergoing a fundamental transformation. Although it is certain that changes are occurring, their extent is questionable. This is even more the case at Nissan, since what we see occurring is a recomposition of the main features of all capitalist enterprises: the need to ensure the appropriation of surplus value. At an organisational level this requires processes of control, surveillance and exploitation of labour.

Nissan's public relations image

> The Nissan car factory in Sunderland is an indication of a new style of industrial relations that has been imported from Japan in recent years. The company, which has Japanese directors but only British workers on the factory floor has attempted to avoid an 'us and them' attitude which is common in manufacturing. There is no traditional division between Nissan 'management' and 'workers'. Everyone uses the same car park and canteen, has the same sickness scheme and perks. There is only one union allowed in the plant—the Amalgamated Engineering Union (AEU), which represents about 35% of the staff. Workers elect representatives to a Company Council to deal with their problems.

> (*The Guardian*, 11 September 1990)

A current vogue among academics and journalists alike is to write of the coming of a 'post-Fordist' society (Murray, 1988; Sayer, 1989). According to this thesis, a 'post-Fordist' society is one in which (among other things) mass production and repetitive, de-skilled working give way to the flexible firm simultaneously capable of delivering more job satisfaction to the 'polyvalent' or multi-skilled employee, and more choice to the customer. In several chapters we remark on the discrepancy that exists between fact and theory as far as the 'post-Fordist' view of industry and society is concerned. As with our intention to look behind the public relations image of Nissan in Sunderland at what actually goes on in the workplace, so we are concerned to establish the empirical evidence for 'post-Fordism' based on our case study. However, the case to be unfolded does not end there. It is not simply a matter of knocking down straw men, but of establishing what it is that makes the Nissan project in Sunderland commercially successful and, importantly, of pinpointing the underlying continuities that allow for the appearance of successful changes. If the sort of lead shown in manufacturing by Nissan (and other Japanese companies) is not due to the claimed revolution in the company ethos, then what is its source? This is the question to be answered in detail by this study, but in the first instance it is appropriate to use a broad brush in setting the context in which the research was undertaken. To do this requires discussion of both the generally important elements of recent industrial change, and also an account of Nissan's corporate development in the business of making and selling motor vehicles.

THE CHALLENGE OF INDUSTRIAL CHANGE

The objective of this book, then, is to address the realities behind the surfaces of industrial change in Britain. We assess the impact which a globally significant multinational car manufacturer is having in a local economy in recession, and from this develop a number of areas of concern. To begin with, a reasonable amount of caution is needed in interpreting the rapidly changing and dynamic nature of local economic developments in Sunderland. Several main questions have already been identified as significant to this analysis (Crowther and Garrahan, 1988), and these throw some initial light on the subject. They include: the extent to which public policy at a national and local level is linked to the direction that industrial change takes; the implications for organised labour of the outcome of these changes; the emergence of corporate business control of the local political environment as part of industrial change; the new relationships that feature between major companies and their suppliers under 'Just-In-Time' (JIT) production systems; the difference between wholesale introduction of JIT and the limited or 'bolt-on' approach; and, finally, the deployment of innovative strategies for human resource management. These points add up to a means of understanding how the human and material relations of production in one local economy are organised so as to maximise Nissan's governance of its corporate identity and business future. In order to operate its production system in a setting in which risks are minimised, Nissan's goal has been to dominate the local economy and control the politics of its development.

Relations with the central and local state are the starting point for contextualising contemporary industrial change in Britain. To judge by its record in Japan and elsewhere in the world's car industry, Nissan shares an ideological affinity with the Thatcher governments over how to deal with organised labour (Cusamano, 1985; Garrahan, 1986; Williamson, 1989). Put simply, the company effectively destroyed the union in a fierce, physical battle in Japan in 1953 which included a lockout of workers and the use by the company of strongarm techniques (Saga, no date; Cusamano, 1985; Armstrong *et al.*, 1985). In Tennessee Nissan benefits from local state laws which champion a 'right to work' charter in employment policies, and thus its plant in Smyrna does not have a union. Although the Nissan workforce in Smyrna was balloted on whether to join the UAW (United Automobile Workers), the company waged a successful campaign against the union. In Sunderland its strategy of a single union deal has helped ensure that union membership is kept down to insignificant levels.

As is the Japanese norm, Nissan employees in Japan are represented by a company union, the elections for which reveal a 'consensus' comparable to the levels displayed by monolithic Stalinist states. For instance, Yamamoto (1980) reports in his study of Nissan in Japan that 99% of employees voted, and that the elected officers of the company council won around 98% of the votes cast, this 'loyalty' deriving 'from the fact that ordinary union members cast their votes under close surveillance' (Yamamoto, 1980, p. 30). As an added boost to this unhealthy arrangement, union officers are generally also employed in the company's personnel department, restricting the chances of workers' views ever being independently represented. Investing in Britain at a time when Thatcherite anti-union legislation was at its height was thus made a lot more comfortable for Nissan. Mrs Thatcher's high regard for the Nissan way of doing things is well known, and not least because Japan long ago achieved her governments' aim of marginalising independent trade unions in industrial and political life.

The Thatcherite, or 'New Right', policy of rolling back the frontiers of the state, at least as far as direct subsidies for manufacturing capital are concerned, has had its counterpart in the opening up of the domestic economy to more direct international investment influence (King, 1987; Massey and Allen, 1988; Overbeek, 1990). So, while established nationalised industries have lost their government support and finance, international private capital has received firm encouragement. This has been especially true where a management style sympathetic to the government's aims was involved, and so both Mrs Thatcher and her close ministerial allies have made visits to Japan to welcome future investment in the British economy. Mrs Thatcher made an important visit to Japan prior to becoming Prime Minister in which she actively sought interviews with the leading figures of Japanese industry. Now the warmth of the government's reception for investment from Japan is clear, as is the fact that Nissan is the former Prime Minister's favourite company. The tragic irony of government policy to run down nationalised industries while welcoming inward investment from abroad in this respect was not lost on the people of Sunderland when Lord Young, as Trade and Industry Minister, celebrated the completion of Nissan's first car built for export in Sunderland in September 1988. Nissan is being underwritten by over £130m in public subsidies to employ some 3500 people directly. At the same time as he was leading the overtures for Nissan, Lord Young's department was initiating what was to become the eventual closure of the sole remaining state-owned shipbuilding firm in Sunderland. North East Shipbuilders was part of the nationalised industry, but unlike most such concerns in the rest of the world, this company and its 2000 employees were refused government grants to continue in existence (Stone, 1988).

The especially warm national welcome offered to investment from Japan by Mrs Thatcher's governments reflects a new direction in economic policy. Increasingly in the 1980s British governments have come under criticism from fellow members of the European Community and from the European Commission itself because of this policy. The ramifications have been felt strongly in the auto industry, recently exemplified by the British government's encouragement—financial or otherwise—for Toyota's investment in Derby, which led to a European Commission investigation of hidden subsidies, and thus unfair competition. Put at its crudest, government policy since 1979 has disavowed state support for industry on grounds of economic sovereignty; and this has applied in high-technology areas as well, as illustrated by the sale of ICL, Britain's only mainframe computer manufacturer, to Fujitsu in July 1990. Where Japan has been able to support three leading mainframe computer manufacturers, Britain is now potentially reduced to the role of onlooker. Government policy appears to be unconcerned that Britain is slipping in the league table of advanced economies:

> What is at issue is whether Britain is to opt out of the strongest growing areas of high technology to become a provider of services and a maker of

low technology goods. It is a policy which City myopia and government indifference are driving us towards fast.

(*The Guardian*, 31 July 1990)

The same newspaper editorial echoed widely held views that it would not be impossible under a different economic regime for Britain to own at least one main-frame computer firm, and the same sentiment could be expressed for the auto industry and other industries.

In contrast with the Conservative reversal under Edward Heath of a similar government policy (then it was called 'no help for lame ducks') that occurred when in 1972 Rolls-Royce was taken into public ownership to avoid bankruptcy, the Conservative governments of the 1980s and early 1990s have unrelentingly stuck to their free market guns. The decline of the manufacturing sector of the British economy is consistently justified by Thatcherites with references to changes in global industry as a whole. In turning their back on what are decried as the 'smokestack industries', UK governments since 1979 have pointed to 'hi-tech' and service sector employment as the way forward. However:

> As much as Thatcherism strives to keep Britain free from foreign inva-
> sions when it comes to refugees from the Third World, it has been more
> than welcoming to foreign economic interests, from the USA and espe-
> cially from Japan. By pursuing such a world-market oriented strategy,
> the structure of Britain's industrial specialisation has come to resemble
> that of semi-peripheral countries, with its specialisation in sectors that
> are not research intensive.

(Overbeek, 1990, p. 214)

The benefits of this 'world-market oriented strategy' are very immediately visible in terms of realising new inward investment. This is especially true when we are speaking of major capital investments by the likes of Fujitsu, Nissan or Toyota, since such inward investment is predicated on expansion. In 1980 the value of Japanese direct investment in the UK economy was $186bn, but by 1989 this had risen to $3956bn. The cumulative total of Japanese direct investment in Europe between 1951 and 1988 stood at $30 164bn, and fully one-third of this entered the UK—mostly during the 1980s (source: Ministry of Finance, Tokyo).

The immediate result of fostering this inflow of capital is that the government can point to new employment which it creates, and after a short time-lag to con-tributions to Britain's export earnings. Over forty years ago, Britain was the world's leading exporter in the auto industry, but after a period of drastic decline the new Japanese investment offers the promise of Britain once again becoming a net exporter of vehicles. The three Japanese companies, Nissan, Toyota and Honda, could be exporting up to half of their combined 500 000 units capacity by the middle of the 1990s. The downside of this policy is self-evident, as all foreign companies investing abroad ultimately share the goal of returning profits to their home base. Ford UK's substantial payments deficit has constantly demonstrated the point. Nevertheless, the positive effect of Japanese car production for export on the UK's balance of trade will be presented as evidence of the success of the policy of opening up the economy to international investment.

NISSAN'S RISE AS A MULTINATIONAL CORPORATION

The Nissan company first had important links with British industry when an agreement was made to produce the Austin A40 Somerset and later Austin A50 Cambridge cars in Japan under licence between 1952 and 1959. 'Austin was chosen as a partner in this effort because of the British company's stability and long history of technological excellence' (source: Nissan Motor Co. Ltd, 1983). The irony of this was not to be lost on the British motor industry, since its virtual eclipse closely followed the dramatic rise of the Japanese car industry to world prominence. Nissan began vigorous pursuit of its international policy from the early 1960s, and now has five major overseas manufacturing plants in Britain, the USA, Mexico, Spain and Australia. Nissan vehicles were first imported into the UK in 1968 and at that time bore the brand name Datsun (DAT being a name derived from the initials of three of the company's first financial backers). The Datsun name was dropped in 1983 as part of the process of standardising the company's varied and expanding global sales under one brand name. The company was already importing 100 000 vehicles into the UK by 1973, and by 1976 it had captured over 6% of the UK market. This growth was restricted from 1975 onwards under the informal agreement which has limited all Japanese imports to 11½% of new vehicle registrations in any one year. The later decision to select Britain as the location for a major European manufacturing platform was undoubtedly influenced by the success Nissan enjoyed in the UK market during the 1970s and 1980s, with the UK having become the company's largest single market outside Japan and the USA. 'Continued trade restrictions in Europe had severely restricted the growth in sales of Nissan vehicles and it had become commercially viable to establish manufacturing facilities within the EEC. Britain, as Nissan's largest market in Europe, was the obvious choice' (source: Nissan Information Pack, 1987).

Of course the name Nissan refers not only to a make of car, but also to the *zaibatsu* or industrial conglomerate characteristic of economic activity in Japan. As one of the newest of the *zaibatsu*, Nissan (which was an abbreviation of Nippon Sangyo, or Japan Industries) has been contrasted with those such as Mitsubishi and Sumitomo, industrial conglomerates formed in earlier centuries. The Nissan Motor Company was orginally established in 1933 under the name Jido-sha Seizo Company, but this was changed to Nissan Motor Company in 1934. With the conclusion of the war in 1945 the industrial conglomerate of which the Nissan Motor Company was part 'included seventy four firms; among the largest were

Hitachi, Nippon Mining, Nissan, and Nissan Chemical' (Cusamano, 1985, p. 28). The 1950s and 1960s were the crucial years for Nissan, since this period saw the transition from a national to a multinational company. An organisational and technological base had been laid during the interwar and wartime years when Nissan, along with other firms, was ordered by the Japanese government to cease production of passenger cars and concentrate on making military vehicles. As the postwar agreement with Austin signified, there was a willingness to engage in the transfer of technology then vital to progressing to volume car production, but the need to introduce new technologies meant that management had to choose between bargaining with labour or challenging its organised voice. In the event, the 1950s became the years when Nissan established its corporate grip on labour-management affairs by confronting and eliminating the basis for independently organised trade unionism amongst its workforce, and setting the pattern of the enterprise or company union which has survived ever since.

Two views of industrial relations at Nissan

Nissan prides itself on 30 years of smooth labour-management relations. The All Nissan Motor Workers' Union was formed in 1953, following a long and acrimonious strike in the same year. Through the experience of this strike, during which all operations were halted for more than four months, both labour and management came to realise the importance of close cooperation. Since the birth of the new union, Nissan has not had another strike, and our employees have contributed to the Company's growth and have been able to enjoy the benefits.

(*Our Global Response: Nissan at Fifty*, Nissan Motor Co. Ltd, 1983)

In an effort to start producing passenger cars, Nissan concluded an agreement in 1952 for a technical tie-up with Austin. The management at Nissan hoped that knockdown assembly of Austin's model would enable their company to learn the skills necessary for passenger car production. In their eyes, however, one serious obstacle clouded Nissan's future: the labour union was staging strikes too frequently and was unwilling to cooperate in production. The workers tried to protect their rights by staging a 100 day strike. In the end, however, they were miserably defeated and the union split. Thus it was by crushing the union that Nissan managed to lay the foundation for its prosperity in the subsequent years.

(Yamamoto, K. (1980) Labour–management relations at Nissan Motor Co. Ltd. *Annals of the Institute of Social Science*, p. 25. University of Tokyo)

On its fiftieth anniversary in 1983, the company's own account of the issue of labour–management affairs declared itself satisfied with the benefits of cooperation which followed the ending of the 1953 strike and the formation of the company's own union. However, other accounts of this industrial conflict and its outcome are at variance with the official version. Management and unions alike were preoccupied with the rebuilding of Japan's economy in the years immediately after 1945 (Johnson, 1982; Okayamo, 1986), but any independent trade union presence after these early years was to be rapidly defeated by management, with the assistance of the US occupying authority (Totsuka, 1982). The tendency towards active state support for what appeared to be a private company policy of attacking trade unionists and removing them from its workforce continued into the 1950s. State intervention 'involved the imposition of a climate of conformism and authoritarian deference, sustained in part by long-term structural underemployment and, especially in the cold-war period of the early 1950s, active interventions to eliminate radical influences in the trade union movement' (Foster and Woolfson, 1989, p. 58).

In 1947 the All-Japan Automobile Workers' Union (AJAWU) signalled the beginning of labour's determination to strengthen its hand in free collective bargaining. Initially, cooperation between management and unions had been motivated by the aim of rescuing companies in the face of the socio-economic upheavals and shortages of the immediate postwar years of occupation and reparation. However, by 1950 the onset of the Korean War caused demand to rise within the Japanese economy, and companies began to resist union pressures. When the AJAWU's members initiated industrial action in 1953, the result was that the strike first collapsed at Toyota and Isuzu, but continued at Nissan, leaving the AJAWU in disarray and subsequent dissolution. Armstrong et al. (1984, p. 190) describe Nissan as having provoked a strike by abandoning wage negotiations in August 1953, and then locking the workers out of the factory and encouraging the formation of a second, company union. As with the rest of the Japanese auto industry, Nissan's control over industrial relations issues became firmly established through the defeat of the independent union and the cementing of the company union. Yamamoto (1980, pp. 28–9) demonstrates that 20 years after defeating the independent union, Nissan's profits had risen 55 fold and that 'workers produced capital which exploited their labour in the subsequent cycle of production at a rate several dozen times or even hundreds of times faster than their wages increased'. There was sustained and dramatic growth in the Japanese economy, illustrated for example by one six-year period between 1955 and 1961 when Japan's business investment increased by 170%, boosting the rate of accumulation from 4% a year to 12% a year (Armstrong et al., 1984, p. 184). Needless to say, this general picture, and the growth of firms such as Nissan in particular, did allow for real wages to rise, but not until the 1960s. After the 1953 strike, Nissan workers first found their pay reduced by 3% a year for six years, and the 1953 pay level was not recovered until 1964 (Cusamano, 1985, p. 167).

In these circumstances at Nissan,

> the moderate enterprise union could always obtain 100% of its annual
> wage claim without any industrial action. This was the result partly of

the restrained claims by the moderate union leaders and partly of the concessions granted and encouragement given these moderate leaders by the company, and also partly due to the fact that favourable market conditions at the time enabled Nissan to afford to grant the wage increases requested.

(Totsuka, 1982, p. 9)

Favourable economic conditions during a period of rapid growth by the company in the 1960s also facilitated the installation by Nissan's management of a system of 'Hanashi Ai' or consultation. The new technologies introduced were discussed via this system before their implementation, and this

seems to have worked well as a kind of buffer to evade the growth of trade union control on the shopfloor. Under this system workers are induced to have an expectation that their complaints or discontent will be 'democratically' dealt with by the consultation bodies

(Totsuka, 1982, p. 9)

So, a favourable economic environment, stable company growth over a long period, the neutralisation of the independent trade union, and the development of a management scheme of prior consultation that minimised the appeal of shop-floor union activity were all factors that helped Nissan to realise the beginning of its self-proclaimed '30 years of smooth labour–management relations'.

The outwardly peaceful industrial relations at Nissan were to be put to the test by the first of the oil crises in 1973, after which domestic demand for cars stagnated, but in any case the close relations between management and union were already attracting adverse comment. These close relations became intermeshed after 1953 through a process of transferring employees between departments. As Cusamano (1985) puts it, 'the union's labour affairs department and the company's personnel department coordinated their activities to the point where, to an outside observer, they seemed almost indistinguishable'. Senior employees in the company's personnel department routinely worked in the company union as part of their career advancement, allowing management direct access to and influence over the union's affairs. This in effect gave Nissan control over the enterprise union, which served different purposes for the company. Following the agreements signed between the company and the union after 1953, employees could be sacked for causing difficulties for the management—for example, if they had affiliations to political groups unacceptable to the company, advocated demo-cratisation of the workplace, or attempted to form a separate union (Cusamano, 1985, p. 416; Saga, no date, p. 11). In addition to assisting Nissan in controlling its workforce, the enterprise union played a vital role in periods when the company's overall performance was cause for concern. The Nissan union uses the slogan of 'the company's prosperity' and is expected to exert its authority to minimise dissent within the workforce. It is clear, then, that collective bargaining by such a company union is largely reduced to a ceremonial status, the union's existence being justified by the company's requirement of disciplining and controlling the workforce so as to enact company policy with the minimum of open criticism or opposition.

This is all a far cry from Nissan's public statement in the celebration of its fiftieth year, and belies the claims made by both the company and the union in Japan of working together with 'mutual trust'. The uncertainties which faced the world auto industry after the 1973 oil crisis were accentuated in Japan, which relies entirely on imported oil. When the domestic demand for cars was adversely affected, Nissan maintained its market position, in which it could depend on union approval. Although the workforce only increased from 50 000 to 56 000 in the 1970s, receipts earned for the company per worker rose from $81 600 in 1970 to $220 400 in 1980. This was achieved with an intensive programme of automation, beginning at the Zama plant making the new Nissan Sunny in 1977. This led to a rise in the organic composition of capital as automation further increased the displacement of living labour in the production process. There followed massive increases in productivity; for example, at the Muryama plant the time taken to produce a vehicle body was reduced by 70% by the end of the 1980s. The emphasis placed on the introduction of robots (at first dedicated or specialised machines, which were replaced in the 1980s with the general-purpose variants allowing more flexibility) needed union backing, and of course at Nissan this came easily. The effects on the workforce were widely felt in that employees were either made redundant, put on temporary contracts, or transferred between as well as within plants to accommodate the installation of robots (Saga, 1983, pp. 3–5).

RESTRUCTURING IN THE WORLD AUTO INDUSTRY

From all the available evidence, there is little to doubt that the world's major manufacturing industries have embarked upon an intensive process of restructuring following the oil-induced recessions of the 1970s and 1980s. Nowhere is this more true than in the auto industry, often characterised as the 'motor of growth' in modern industrial society as a whole (Altshuler et al., 1984). Thus, if the demand for motor vehicles stops rising, this is traditionally seen as an indication of a slowing down of the economy; likewise, if demand drops and the industry finds itself in a crisis of over-production, as it did in the mid-1980s, there follows a cumulative and damaging impact on the rest of the economy. The historical tendency for capitalist economies to veer from boom to recession, with periodic crises of failing to match consumption with production is inevitably reflected in the fortunes of the auto industry. This, the largest of the world's industries, has also become the arena of massive profitability coupled with corporate collapse, takeovers and concentration of ownership. The epithet 'Car Wars' seems hardly out of place for an industry in which survival is often determined by having to grow in a stagnant or shrinking market (notwithstanding the growth potential that now exists in Eastern Europe). It is this which has also led to the necessity for some companies either to increase market share at the expense of competitors through their own forceful expansion, or to join forces in shared ventures, or part-mergers. This ongoing process is not confined to the giant auto firms, but is a feature of the entire industry; it thus also affects components firms making original equipment for supply to the vehicle assemblers and to the after-sales market (Amin and Smith, 1990).

'Car Wars' and the concentration of ownership

> Behind the glossy adverts and the dependable image of the car makers, the world's largest industry is being shaken to its foundations. But in the midst of the Car Wars the world is being taken apart and put together again to suit the needs of the strongest combatants. Opportunistic alliances are unexpectedly formed, some to test the strength of an opponent, others as a scarcely disguised prelude to the stronger gobbling up the weaker. . . . National economic strategies, even Europe-wide strategies, remain subservient to the multi-billion dollar assaults being launched from the boardrooms of General Motors, Ford, Toyota, Nissan, Peugeot, VW, and Fiat. . . . What we are witnessing is the permanent and global restructuring of the key manufacturing sector within western capitalism.

> (Bill Ridgers, *The Nissan Factor*, mimeograph, May 1985)

The MIT study of 'The Future of the Automobile' (Altshuler *et al.*, 1984) showed that productivity in Japanese auto firms outstripped US and European competitors in the 1960s and 1970s, but that several factors contributed to this competitive edge. There is considerable agreement, for example, about three factors which were important then: the Japanese government's policy of deliberately restraining the value of the yen which, in a weakened condition, gave a built-in cost advantage to Japanese exports; the absence for the most part of anything other than voluntary restrictions on Japanese imports to the USA and Western Europe; and the strong support from the state in Japan, via the Ministry of International Trade and Investment (MITI), for Japanese auto firms, both vehicle assemblers and components suppliers, seeking overseas markets. In sum, the role of the state in the Japanese auto industry, as in other industries, had been instrumental: the strength of individual firms could not be isolated from the direct and indirect steps taken by governments and other agencies to assist manufacturing enterprises in promoting their exports. In just this way, the state came to play a significant role in assisting those companies transferring production overseas in the 1980s, both to overcome the obstacle to exports as the yen strengthened and to beat the rising tide of protectionism—associated in particular with the advent after 1992 of the Single European Market, but also feared from the USA, given the severe imbalance of trade between the USA and Japan.

The intercontinental movement of capital in the auto industry reflected in the transplanting of auto production from Japan to North America and Western Europe is one element in a broader trend across the whole of the Japanese economy. Data from the Japan External Trade Organisation (*The Guardian*, 31 July 1990) show that Japanese companies invested about $4 billion abroad in 1982, but five years later the same amount was going into foreign markets quarterly, and by 1990 the figure was $4 billion monthly. For most of the postwar years world markets have been dominated by US-owned companies, but the accelerating level of Japanese investment overseas is an indicator of how the balance of global economic forces is changing. To take the North-East of England as an example of a recipient region in global capital restructuring, there was only one Japanese manufacturing company in the region when Mrs Thatcher first took up residence in Downing Street in 1979; now there are more than three dozen, and their number increases regularly. The more than 130 Japanese-controlled companies now in business in the UK directly employ around 30 000 people, but whereas US-owned companies operating in the UK have forty times as many British employees, the significance lies in the fact that Japanese capital is expanding its interest in Britain while US companies withdraw in the face of global competition from Japan. In parts of the UK like the North-East, where traditional industries have declined and been discarded as smokestack industries, the reshaping of global competition between US and Japanese capital comes as a mixed blessing. Growing interest in the region during the 1980s by Japanese firms has produced thousands of new jobs, but during the same period many US companies have run down their operations or withdrawn from the region completely. The evidence for this debate is examined in more detail in Chapter 2, but before then we must outline the impact on the US auto industry of inward investment from Japan in order to set the context for Nissan's own plans for expansion as a global manufacturing enterprise.

THE FIRST WAVE OF JAPANESE AUTO TRANSPLANTS: THE USA

It is against the background of these far-reaching upheavals that we have seen the demise of the USA as the world's dominant economic force. By contrast, Japanese capital is ahead of the field in switching the geographical location of production so as to profit from new world markets. For Nissan and the other giant auto manufacturers in the domestic Japanese motor vehicle market, the relative lack of growth and consequent declining profits at home were factors which, combined with a substantial surplus of capital accumulated from the halcyon days of the 1970s, pointed companies firmly in the direction of overseas production. Initially, of course, the phenomenal success of Japanese auto firms in the early 1970s meant they could supply their overseas markets from production platforms in Japan; but from the late 1970s onwards there has been a radical shift to a policy of foreign direct investment aimed at the world's two major auto markets outside Japan, the USA and the European Community. This policy manifested itself in two over-lapping waves during this time, beginning first in North America and turning then to Western Europe. In sum, this policy has helped overcome the cost to Japanese manufacturers which the strengthening of the yen increasingly imposed on them during this time, and it has also provided the means of circumventing trade barriers already in place, or anticipated after 1992.

Japanese imported vehicle sales grew steadily throughout the 1960s and 1970s until by 1980 they had come to account for 27% of the US market. Quota restric-tions of 2.3 million imports a year from Japan were introduced to protect the USA's own auto industry from any further deterioration in its domestic standing, and the seriousness of the situation was illustrated by the fact that in 1980 General Motors experienced its first annual loss for over half a century. Ironically, the effect of the quotas was to encourage Japanese companies to relocate their produc-tion operations to the USA in the form of transplants or joint venture companies. In the USA individual state governments have the responsibility, emphasised under the Reagan administrations, for promoting the economic development of their areas. They have welcomed Japanese firms wanting to establish 'trans-plants' with an array of grants, subsidies and tax concessions, and the seven major Japanese firms took up the option of setting up transplants in the USA during the 1980s: Honda in 1982, Nissan in 1983, Mazda in 1987, Mitsubishi in 1988—in a joint venture with Chrysler named Diamond Star, Toyota in 1988, and Subaru/ Isuzu in a joint venture in 1989. In addition, Toyota and General Motors embarked on a joint venture in 1984 called NUMMI (New United Motor Manu-facturers Inc.). During the 1980s, then, investments in the USA and Canada by the seven leading Japanese auto companies marked a transfer of production equal in size to the whole of the current market for new vehicles in the UK. This sudden and dramatic increase in capacity within the USA necessarily precipitated a crisis of over-production, a crisis from which the three major US companies, General Motors, Ford and Chrysler—known as the 'Big Three'—have been the predict-able losers.

The collapse in the fortunes of the US auto industry was as rapid as it was dramatic: in the mid-1950s up to two-thirds of world motor vehicle production is estimated to have occurred in the USA, but decline was already beginning ten to fifteen years later as vehicles began to be imported from abroad in large numbers. There followed a decade of losing out to foreign, especially Japanese, imports in the 1970s, especially when the cost of fuel escalated after the oil crisis and tradi-tional 'over-sized gas-guzzlers' lost out in preference to 'down-sized fuel-efficient' foreign imports. Thus, by 1980 'the US auto industry experienced the worst economic downturn in its post-World War II history. The auto giants lost a combined $3.5 billion; 250 000 workers went on indefinite layoff; and an addi-tional 450 000 were unemployed in the industries that supply the Big Three'

(Hill, 1984, p. 142). The recession which continued between 1979 and 1982 saw a falling rate of profit for the Big Three and there followed extensive plant closures throughout the country.

If the 1970s were the years of US auto firms falling behind in the face of competition from imports, the story of the 1980s is of intense domestic competition for sales between the Big Three and the Japanese manufacturers newly established in the mid-western and southern states. At the start of the decade the USA's own auto firms were already shaken by the market penetration of imported vehicles and so could claim only 84% of sales where they had once dominated; by the end of the 1980s that figure was down to 68%, with Japanese companies accounting for a quarter of all sales (*The Independent*, 6 November 1989). Although General Motors retained its status as the world's single largest corporation, the US auto industry as a whole faces the prospect of its decline continuing into the 1990s mainly as a result of being outpaced by Japanese competition. A substantial restructuring process geared to responding to this competition is under way, and in the process Japanese and US firms have entered into more and more extensive joint operations. From the point of view of the US companies this is seen as a cheap way of participating in technology transfer, for example at NUMMI, Diamond Star and Ford-Isuzu. For Japanese companies this is an effective way to secure import penetration.

Many older plants belonging to US companies have been subject to closure, since the sales of Ford, Chrysler and General Motors vehicles assembled in the USA have on the whole fallen. At the same time, there has been a steady increase in the share of the US market being taken by Japanese vehicles assembled in the USA. In the first half of 1990, Japanese vehicles accounted for 28% of all car sales in the USA and the Big Three saw their combined share of the market decline again to 65%. With General Motors and Ford taking 36.2% and 21.1% of the market respectively, Chrysler now has the same sales as Toyota at 9%, with Nissan just behind at 8%. This is happening at a time when the US demand for new vehicles is levelling off, with the 1989 total of 9.8 million new car registrations being again below the high point of over 10.5 million in the mid-1980s.

When the first major wave of foreign direct investment from Japanese auto firms and from associated companies supplying components concentrated on North America, a twofold pattern emerged in which plants set up by major Japanese vehicle assemblers were followed very soon by investments from Japanese components manufacturers. This pattern established itself in several states, such as Indiana, Illinois, Michigan and Ohio, stretching from the Great Lakes southwards through Kentucky to Tennessee, the state in which Nissan's Smyrna development is situated (Mair *et al.*, 1988; Rubenstein, 1987, 1988). It is estimated that around 300 Japanese components firms set up production in the USA in the ten-year period ending in 1991, and once again the evidence is that MITI (the Japanese government's ministry for assisting overseas investments) continued to play a strong part both in providing state financial support and in directing components firms to specific areas of the USA where Japanese auto firms needed them (Reid, 1989). The tendency for Japanese components suppliers to cluster around the large Japanese auto firms in the USA compares with similar cases involving the setting up of other subcontracting complexes, for example in the European electronics industry (Morris, 1987). In south Wales the inflow of investment from Japanese electronics firms clearly signified this development, and as elsewhere the question to be asked regards the extent to which components are locally sourced.

If large Japanese firms do not draw on locally sourced components from existing indigenous suppliers, the critical issue is to what extent is the investment making a significant contribution to the local economy. As the more detailed discussion of this issue in Chapter 2 makes plain, the degree to which the host economy can benefit from major inward investment can be measured by the stimulus for growth which is injected into local manufacturing industries. If the subcontracting complex is transferred substantially intact from Japan, it is hard to avoid the conclusion that the host economy is providing no more than the land and the labour, sweetened with government development grants, with reduced benefit to domestic economic growth and prosperity. If depressed local and regional manufacturing industries in the UK are to plan for a growth trajectory on the basis of foreign inward investment, something more must be achieved than this worst-case scenario which has led at least one prominent British politician to condemn the developing situation as akin to 'economic colonialism'. Reactions to this process of 'economic colonialism' in the USA have invariably been mixed and some attempts at reversing the declining sales of US vehicles have been made using dubious appeals to patriotism. The Rockefeller Center in New York was sold in 1989 to a Japanese property company, and one media campaign dubbed this the 'Hirohito Center' as part of its message that preferring Japanese goods over US ones was unpatriotic. This media advertising has also been allowed to take on an overtly racist message with the recent broadcasting of a television commercial in which US citizens were encouraged to buy cars 'built for our size families, not theirs' (*Financial Times*, 18 September 1990). The most worrying aspect for marketing departments is that customers tend to develop a brand loyalty, and a whole generation of US car owners has now grown up accustomed to buying Japanese cars. The Honda Accord is now the best-selling model in the USA. While US media campaigns do not flinch from resorting to these offensively racist messages, the lesson being learnt by car salespersons is that Japanese imports and Japanese vehicles made in the USA maintain their popularity with customers. The US auto firms themselves have been responding in several more constructive ways, most notably by imitating what are considered the essential features of the Japanese achievements in obtaining higher levels of productivity: as we indicated above, this is being done both by entering joint ventures with Japanese firms as a means in the short term of maintaining sales, and by introducing Japanese management practices into their own existing and planned manufacturing operations in the long term. General Motors has a one-third share in Isuzu, Ford has a one-quarter share in Mazda, Chrysler has a 15% interest in

Mitsubishi, and so on. This interpenetration of capital is accompanied by cooperative agreements, such as that by which Ford assembles light vans for Nissan, and this sort of cooperation is on the increase. While these different arrangements offer US companies some sort of lifeline, they also constitute further avenues by which Japanese companies can gain access to the US market.

A question of state support for private capital

> Fujitsu's planned $400m move to Newton Aycliffe in County Durham [in North East England] would not have arisen if normal market forces had been left to take their course. I think we have to recognise that investment would not have taken place if we had left everything to market forces. The reason the Japanese are here is because it is the only way that they can gain access to the European market. Let us not say it is a huge vote of confidence, it is part of economic colonisation. The sun is rising for the rising sun of investment—that is what Japanese investment means in world terms. If it makes such obvious sense for Fujitsu to invest in the North East, why can our government not invest in ship-building in the North East.
>
> (Bryan Gould, Labour Opposition spokesperson on Industry, April 1989, from a speech to the Tom Cordner Press Awards in Sunderland)

However, while the Big Three US auto firms strive to reconstruct their design and production methods to compete more successfully with Japanese companies, the latter continue to profit from carefully calculated decisions about the location of their production facilities. Japanese transplants have concentrated on finding locations in the mid-western or upper-southern states of the USA, roughly along the route of Interstate Highway 75 from Michigan to Tennessee. But within this general pattern there are more specific threads to be highlighted. In particular, the choice of locations is largely though not exclusively confined to those providing greenfield sites in areas without significant ethnic minorities in their local labour markets. Small towns have been preferred and where the seven major auto firms have gone, four out of five of the more than 300 Japanese components firms operating in the USA have followed. These seven major firms have each sited their plants in different states, and of these Nissan was the one to select a state with so-called 'right to work' legislation, which eliminates free trade union organisation within plants. Overall, therefore, Japanese firms have sought out locations where the workforce is 'not imbued with traditional union values and work practices and hence will be more amenable to accepting the new production techniques and management practices' (Reid, 1989, p. 49).

The public relations slant on the choice of these locations typically stresses the low cost of land and the improved working environment in greenfield sites away from congested urban centres. But the importance which Japanese companies themselves place on industrial relations leaves little reason to doubt that labour considerations were of primary importance. The spatial clustering of supplier firms around the final vehicle assemblers is determined significantly by the need for close geographical proximity in the operation of Just-In-Time systems central to Japanese methods (Schoenberger, 1987; Gertler, 1988). Of course, the components firms then also benefit from the same pliable labour market as the seven large auto firms they supply.

THE SECOND WAVE OF JAPANESE AUTO TRANSPLANTS: EUROPE

The EC automobile industry has been in a state of almost constant commercial upheaval throughout the 1980s and this looks likely to continue into the immediate future. The EC has strengthened its own interventionist role with agreements by the member states to begin setting up the single market, and therefore the EC has naturally concentrated much attention on this fundamentally important industry. Official estimates are that one in ten jobs in the EC economy depend directly or indirectly on the automobile sector, taking into account the direct employment of 1.7m people by car firms as well as the additional jobs in the suppliers, car dealerships, garage repairs and other related services. The central position of the auto industry is illustrated by the fact that it achieves 29% of the total EC balance of trade in manufactured goods, its success being vital also for the steel, rubber, plastic and other basic industries from which it draws materials (European Commission, 1989).

Given its central economic position, the EC optimistically anticipated that the liberalisation of trading among member states after 1992 would generate growth in the industry. In essence, the EC view is that the removal of fiscal, physical and technical barriers to internal EC trade will ultimately generate economies of scale and lower costs to the producers, greater industry-wide profits, and thus benefits to the consumer in terms of lower prices resulting from free competition (Ludvigsen Associates, 1988). These supposed advantages can only accrue if the growth depicted in the economic modelling used by the European Commission comes about (Cecchini, 1988). There are sceptical views on the wider growth forecasts for the EC following 1992, however (Hall and Wilson, 1989). Indeed, no evidence is offered by the EC for where the growth will occur and, therefore, which member states or regions of the EC will benefit or lose.

This doubt about the future affects the configuration that the European auto industry will take during the last decade of the twentieth century. It comes on top of the greater apprehension that there will be little immediate growth in intra-European motor vehicle trade except for the Japanese and the German producers. The forecasts used by the Commission to justify the free-market economy after 1992 have been subject to particularly stringent and damaging criticism (Cutler *et al.*, 1989). The EC's starting assumption is that there is a relatively easy route to be followed which will achieve the advantages to both consumers and producers outlined above. The major indigenous European firms are Fiat, VW, Peugeot and Renault, and these four together take just over half of the sales within the EC market. When calculated along with the sales of the smaller manufacturers such as Rover, Mercedes-Benz and BMW, the share of the EC market held by indigenous companies comes to around two-thirds. Approximately another quarter of the market is accounted for by the sales of the two long-established US companies, Ford and GM, and so the existing auto industry would seem to be in a strong position to prosper from the single European market given that it already has slightly under nine out every ten new vehicle registrations in any one year. However, the removal of barriers to intra-European trade will be of just as much benefit to Japanese transplants as to the existing firms in the industry configuration just described. More worrying still for indigenous companies is that in all likelihood it will be of even greater benefit to those Japanese firms opening up volume manufacturing within the EC in the late 1980s and early 1990s because they are the industry leaders in efficiency and productivity.

It is this combination of circumstances threatening to destabilise the indigenous EC manufacturers which has marked the much heralded coming of free trade after 1992. That only the strong (or the subsidised) will survive the continuing upheavals in the global auto industry, and indeed that there will be such upheavals in the face of sustained competition from Japanese transplants within the EC following the single market after 1992, is widely accepted. In order to cope with the jointly pressing issues of 1992 and competition from Japanese transplants, as well as the enduring longer-term problem of overcapacity, the EC's own auto industry has been forced into a restructuring process along lines similar to that in the USA. Within Britain and the rest of Europe major producers are anxiously seeking, or being sought for, partnership with other manufacturers both domestically and globally. Rover's joint ventures with Honda, the joint production of Iveco trucks by Ford and Fiat, General Motors' controlling share of Saab, the Renault investment in Volvo, and Ford's outright purchase of Jaguar are examples of this development mirroring the shared undertakings previously seen in the USA as the world auto industry goes through the present period of reconstruction and concentration of ownership. Cooperative agreements between producers are flourishing, and while the major indigenous EC firms have yet to enter into complete mergers, the process of establishing links between major and minor firms has already begun. Nevertheless, the industry's instability unquestionably remains unresolved, since overall capacity still stands at around 14 million units, while demand has levelled off at about 12 million at the start of the 1990s. A further area of doubt is the extent of sustained demand from the new markets opening up in Eastern Europe.

The building of larger agglomerations of companies as a defence against the vagaries of the market is a strategy pursued with rather more vigour (and success) by some companies than others; in Nissan's case it has largely been a case of going it alone. The second major surge in the Japanese-led restructuring of world motor vehicle production was targeted on the European Community countries and began when investment in North America was already under way. Having secured substantial production facilities in the USA, Nissan was the first Japanese auto firm to gain access to the European market with a transplant facility of similar size to that laid down in the USA. With this move across the Atlantic, Nissan's European strategy turned out to be primarily a UK strategy in the first instance. Nissan's corporate plan in the 1980s has been to seek out greenfield sites for its sole development, first in Smyrna in Tennessee and then in Sunderland. The objective of setting up operations within the European Community car market is one shared by several of the major Japanese auto manufacturers. But this strategy is not just about overcoming the tariff barriers against foreign imports to forestall any increase after 1992. It is also very much a means of surviving in a world motor vehicle industry which is certain to see further concentration of ownership as less competitive companies are compelled into mergers or subjected to takeovers. Nissan does not intend to be in this position, and the plant recently opened in Sunderland is evidence of a strategy to increase, not simply maintain, Nissan's penetration of the UK and European markets.

NISSAN IN SUNDERLAND

In the last thirty years the rise of Nissan and other Japanese auto manufacturers has seen them become leading companies worldwide, matched in output only by the US giants General Motors and Ford. Whereas in 1960 General Motors and Ford ranked first and second in production, with no Japanese companies counted among the top ten in the world, by the early 1980s the two US leaders faced Toyota and Nissan in third and fourth position respectively (Dicken, 1986, p. 297). Nissan made 2.7 million vehicles in 1988 and possibly aims to sell up to 3 million vehicles a year by the mid-1990s. Quite apart from its global standing in terms of the number of vehicles sold every year, however, the notable feature of Nissan's strategy has been the decision to switch to foreign-based manufacturing. As a result, Nissan has plants in almost two dozen countries, and (like other major auto firms) now has its sights set on an Eastern European development. The first of Nissan's transplants, i.e. local production overseas, was established in Mexico, and others followed in Australia, Spain and so on. By 1988, Nissan was making 88 000 vehicles annually at its facility in Mexico, 58 000 in Spain and 43 000 in Australia (source: Nissan Annual Report, 1988). The Smyrna, Tennessee, and Sunderland transplants proved distinctive in this policy because of their greenfield sites, and also because of the size of their investments and the consequent plant capacities. The Smyrna plant was producing 217 000 vehicles by 1988, and at Sunderland production rose from 9000 to 77 000 vehicles between 1987 and 1990; output of 200 000 per annum is projected at Sunderland after 1992. Each of these transplants has an estimated capacity of half a million vehicles. Since both the US and UK plants were developed during the 1980s they represent a major accentuation of an existing overseas investment strategy which Nissan had been following

for most of the previous two decades. Although Nissan's policy of overseas production dates back to the 1960s, when the first transplant was set up in Mexico,
the 1980s has seen a quantum leap in this policy. Thus, it is worth asking what
were the circumstances which propelled the company's strategy of setting up a
complete local production process in Western Europe.

In the annual report for the fiscal year ending in March 1988, Nissan recorded
the total value of its worldwide vehicle sales at $22.3 billion. Total sales for the
company, also taking into account diversified operations like aerospace equipment, textile machinery, industrial machinery and marine products, amounted to
$27.3 billion, or approximately the same amount as for the previous fiscal year.
Importantly, the sale of Nissan vehicles in Japan exceeded exports for the first
time in nine years. This reflects the company's relatively poor performance in the
1980s in the Japanese market, and indeed Williamson (1989) observes that unlike
Toyota, its major competitor in Japan, Nissan has relied heavily on exports:
typically during the 1980s exports accounted for just over 50% of Nissan's production, but only 40% of Toyota's. While Toyota has remained the dominant
company in Japan, Nissan has seen its share of the domestic market during most
of the 1980s remain level or fall. Indeed in 1982, events seemed to take a turn for
the worse for the whole Japanese auto industry. After over three decades of annual
increases, exports fell for the first time in 1982, and domestic production saw its
first annual decrease for a decade. The subsequent prominence of the strong yen
in the 1980s has turned the reliance of Nissan and other Japanese auto manufacturers on exports into a negative influence on companies' foreign currency transactions, making an even stronger case for switching from the export of vehicles
made in Japan to local production overseas. Nissan's own domestic achievements
have continued to go badly towards the end of the decade, with its market share
in Japan falling from about 20% in 1984 to under 18% in 1988 (Williamson,
1989, pp. 6-7). The attractions of a major investment inside the European
Community—potentially the world's single biggest car market with 320 million
people—immune from trade barriers, thus became compelling: making the
vehicles closer to the customers would reduce transport costs; a cheap and large
supply of labour was available, especially in the depressed regions; and government development grants would diminish the initial costs of setting up a major
production operation by up to one-third. This is what the UK had to offer, backed
up by government policies against organised labour which were the harshest in
Western Europe.

Nissan's own forecasts for growth

It is essential that we achieve a large scale of production if we are to
ensure our company as a major auto maker in the global arena. In order
to promote the sustained growth of our company as a truly international
enterprise, we at Nissan have positioned overseas production as one of
our mainstay corporate activities, along with domestic sales and exports

of finished vehicles. We hope to realise overseas production of 1 million units and finished vehicle exports of 1.5 million units in the early 1990s.

(Overseas Production Activities, Nissan Information Pack, 1984)

Nissan is moving towards the objective of securing a ten percent share of the worldwide market by the early 1990s.

(Nissan Annual Report, 1984)

TOWARDS FLEXIBILITY AND TEAMWORKING

A number of issues are encountered when we turn to the question of why Nissan chose to invest in a plant in Britain, as opposed to another member of the European Community such as Spain (which has had Europe's fastest-growing auto industry in the latter part of the 1980s). As already indicated, Nissan's preference for the UK was determined significantly by the previous success of its products with the British car-buying public, and also by the sympathies which the Thatcher governments displayed towards Japanese management practices and anti-union attitudes. The inducements to inward investment offered by individual countries were taken into account, as well as the attractions of the final choice of a particular local economy in which to build the manufacturing facility. Any multinational company embarking on an overseas investment of the size of Nissan's in Sunderland (in excess of £650 million) will attempt to minimise the risks, especially as the whole object of the venture is to secure the company's future in an unstable and highly competitive market. Although a giant manufacturer by British standards, Nissan is known in Japan as the 'hibernating elephant' for its sluggish performance against domestic competition (Williamson, 1989). The Nissan complex in Sunderland has profound importance for the present and future condition of Britain's motor vehicle market. In addition, Nissan has chosen to reproduce to a high level in Sunderland both the material and the social conditions perfected in Japan for corporate control of the entire production process. This radical approach in turn means that Nissan maximises its corporate power over organised labour, over components suppliers, over land use control, over public authorities, in effect over the entire local economy. What is occurring in practice is the subordination of much of the local polity and economy to the interests of a single company, vividly demonstrating the impact of global capital movements on a given locality. More than many other localities in the UK, Sunderland epitomises the local effects of the contemporary restructuring of the country's industrial geography. Sunderland has been beset by far-reaching de-industrialisation after many decades of relative and gradual decline (Stone and Stevens, 1988). The local economy is now subject to something of a limited resurgence of industrial activity in which Nissan plays the leading role (Hudson, 1989; Garrahan and Stewart, 1991a; Amin and Tomaney, forthcoming).

As well as empathising politically and industrially with the right-wing ideas of contemporary British governments, Nissan joins hands with the local authorities to 'create jobs for local people'. As a result, Nissan, like any other foreign company involved in inward investment, is cast in the role of benefactor and shares a unity of purpose with both central and local arms of the state. Similar examples of this development have been documented elsewhere, notably in south Wales (Morgan and Sayer, 1988). Local councils in the North-East of England have been dominated by Labour, albeit right-of-centre or labourist, politics for most of this century. However, an apparent consensus between Nissan and the elected Labour local authorities is dictated by the latter's electoral need to be seen to be responding to high rates of unemployment. The effect is that Labour councils face a dilemma: they must cooperate closely with a company which brings employment to a depressed area, even though they know that this will mean a largely de-unionised workforce; this latter perspective is kept off the public agenda. As we show in Chapter 2, the consequence of this situation is a company-imposed consensus; whether a transformation was either necessary or desirable in the area's traditional industrial and cultural life, in which collective labour representation played a key part, has been ignored. Ultimately, it has never been asked whether local economic development should be premised on the decline of organised labour. In view of the data presented in Chapters 3 and 4, this is an issue calling out for attention, both academic and public.

In its approach to organised labour, Nissan offered a single-union agreement on a non-negotiable basis, ultimately signing with the Amalgamated Engineering Union. The interpretation we place on this in later chapters is that Nissan intended to marginalise, if not to eclipse completely, the role and influence of unions in the daily industrial life of its workforce. This concern with establishing unfettered control extends beyond the human relations of production to control over the physical environment and relations with supplier companies. Another condition for the Nissan investment was that the company would secure sufficient land for its development purposes; as a result the company now owns 733 acres of the Borough of Sunderland. This gives Nissan effective industrial development control both over the physical environment and over its favoured trading partners, since Nissan does not need all of this 733 acres for itself, but is engaging in onward sales to supplier companies. The local council retains the nominal status of planning authority, but since it is Nissan which decides on onward sales, the company's control over the physical environment is heightened and so, by implication, is Nissan's superior relationship over its components suppliers.

While the determination of land use enhances the vertical integration between Nissan and components suppliers, it is also vital to the efficiency of the 'Just-In-Time' (JIT) production process. Suppliers located in the immediate vicinity of the Nissan plant will facilitate the JIT system by being within short delivery time of the main factory. In addition to this we see at Nissan other components of JIT such as 'pull-through' rather than 'push-through' production arrangements, minimal inventories and total quality management on the line. In short, these are attempts to manage out uncertainty at source in each part of the production cycle. Those suppliers that are on land bought from Nissan are also replicating Nissan's policy of de-unionising the workforce to eliminate obstacles to the management of the JIT system. In the JIT system of manufacturing, the major steps in the production process are being brought together in Sunderland and the surrounding area in a spatially concentrated way. This distinguishes it from most established European auto manufacturing platforms, which tend to disperse the main steps in production to different geographical locations, bringing them together only for the final assembly.

The Sunderland development also sets Nissan apart from the increasing, but otherwise partial, emulation of the JIT system elsewhere in British industry (Sayer, 1986). Nissan's operation of the JIT method is far from the refined versions of this to be found in the likes of 'Toyota City' in Japan, but it is the most extensive variant of its kind yet in Britain or in Europe as a whole (Sheard, 1983; Hill, 1987; Mair *et al.*, 1988). The risks in this venture are high, and by locating such high levels of the production process in one location Nissan has been obliged to devise a corporate strategy to control that location. As we show in Chapter 2, this is indeed happening in Sunderland, and Nissan is in an unchallenged position in the local economy. It sits atop an organisational pyramid creating the conditions in which the JIT system works most effectively, and in which Nissan can effectively direct the development, design, pricing and delivery of components by supplier companies. In addition, the policy of playing down the role of unions in supplier companies is also achieved by Nissan's domination of the situation.

Nevertheless, the central issue remains whether these major changes to the organisation of manufacturing can work now that unions have been relegated to the place of onlooker. If the Nissan project is a success, is this because of the more scientific and rational principles on which its system is based, and has the company achieved the significant feat of redirecting popular attitudes to the experience of working in manufacturing? Our argument is that Nissan does represent another way of doing things in industry, and that it is far more than in-situ change. However, what we aim to show in the rest of this book is that success has its costs. The Nissan investment marks a radical departure from past, and decidedly less systematic, versions of vehicle assembly in the UK or Europe. But the public image which the company has been able to project so far is of a contented workforce enjoying the fruits of becoming more skilled in their work, deriving more job satisfaction, and living through a revolution in industrial attitudes. We want to open the debate about the wider social and industrial implications of this claim, and to consider carefully the desirable and undesirable effects of trying to manufacture a new industrial culture. We do this in the following chapters by focusing initially on the impact of the Nissan investment on the North-East, and then drawing on interviews with Nissan employees to examine the notions of flexibility and teamworking which allegedly are the key to achieving a revival of competitiveness in British manufacturing.

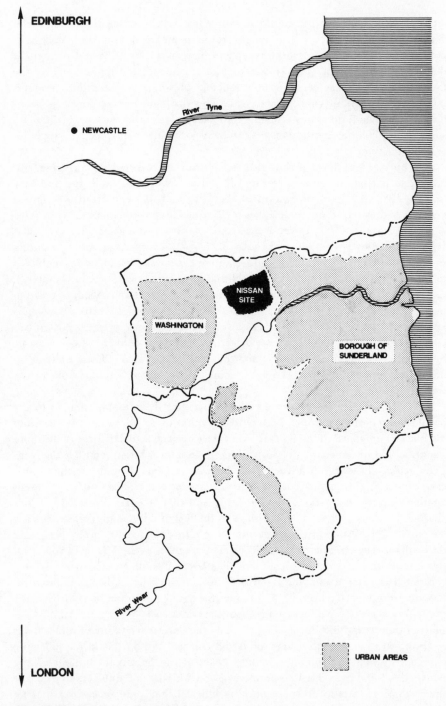

EDINBURGH

● NEWCASTLE

River Tyne

NISSAN SITE

WASHINGTON

BOROUGH OF SUNDERLAND

River Wear

LONDON

URBAN AREAS

Figure 2 The Nissan site in Sunderland.

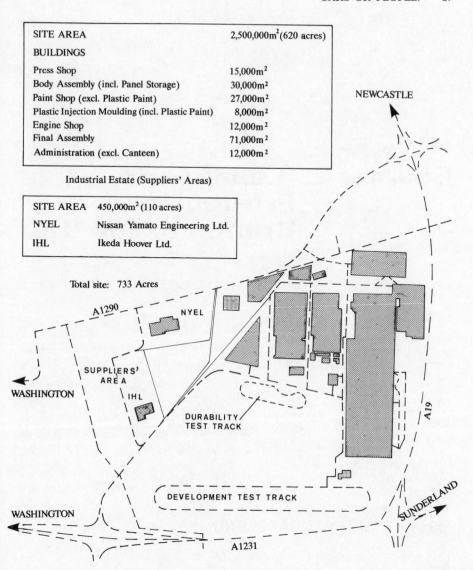

SITE AREA	2,500,000m² (620 acres)
BUILDINGS	
Press Shop	15,000m²
Body Assembly (incl. Panel Storage)	30,000m²
Paint Shop (excl. Plastic Paint)	27,000m²
Plastic Injection Moulding (incl. Plastic Paint)	8,000m²
Engine Shop	12,000m²
Final Assembly	71,000m²
Administration (excl. Canteen)	12,000m²

Industrial Estate (Suppliers' Areas)

SITE AREA	450,000m² (110 acres)
NYEL	Nissan Yamato Engineering Ltd.
IHL	Ikeda Hoover Ltd.

Total site: 733 Acres

NEWCASTLE

A1290

NYEL

SUPPLIERS' AREA

WASHINGTON

IHL

DURABILITY TEST TRACK

A19

DEVELOPMENT TEST TRACK

SUNDERLAND

WASHINGTON

A1231

Figure 3 The Nissan site area.

Chapter 2: 'Lean' Auto Production Comes to the UK

The entire Japanese auto industry in 1950 produced only 30 000 vehicles —about one and a half days' production in the United States.

(Cusamano, 1985, p. 266)

By the year 2000 Japanese companies could be producing around 1.7 million cars and 250 000 mainly light, commercial vehicles in Western Europe, of which 1 million could be made by Nissan, Toyota, Honda, and others in the UK.

(NCC, 1990, p. 19)

NISSAN AND THE LOCAL ECONOMY

The socio-cultural as well as economic relationships between depressed localities and multinational firms investing in them will always be of relevance to an understanding of capitalist society. They tell us about the powerful forces for change in modern capitalism; but often the construction of a cooperative spirit between local communities and incoming multinational employers serves to conceal certain key elements. The important decision-making power is still reserved by the private investing 'partner' in local economic development issues, especially as mobile investment has plenty of choice between the declining areas in a country with recent experience of recession like the UK. Localities winning out in the beauty contest to attract inward investment from private companies also act as the grateful recipients of this investment and the jobs it brings, but leaders of the local

business and public sector have their own political reasons for representing themselves and their groups as positive and instrumental actors in the process. They
can claim credit for producing employment against the previous tide of company
closures and redundancies. This interplay has been a common feature of local
economic development in the post-World War II period in the UK, with the
exception of attempts at more *dirigiste* intervention by some left-wing Labour local
councils in the 1980s (Cochrane, 1989). The reality for the most part is that the
bigger the investing company, the more power and influence it can exert over
localities in the free-market competition encouraged by recent British government
policy. Nevertheless, the decision by Nissan to invest in Sunderland was hailed as
a major local victory, involving beating off contenders and successfully convincing
Nissan of the greater desirability of the Sunderland location as opposed to the
dozens of others in the country which put in bids for the development.

However, the fact of bringing a giant multinational company to the North-East
of England to open the region's first major auto plant had other consequences for
the local economy, much more significant than were immediately evident in the
euphoria of the announcement. When it chose Sunderland, Nissan was fêted not
just locally but nationally as representing the new age of 'lean' production, which
held the promise of future prosperity. The emphasis was on teamworking, flexibility and quality, and Nissan's high levels of proven productivity were 'lean'
because they used fewer material and human resources for more efficient output.
The message put across was that since Nissan could be expected to be a progressive as well as an efficient alternative to the wasteful and soon-to-be-discarded local
industrial tradition, a process of modernisation would surely follow in which other
companies with similar prospects would be attracted into the area. Because of this,
the Nissan investment in Sunderland was hailed as the start of a new episode in the
regeneration of the local economy and its surrounding subregion. This was a
view emphasised by Mrs Thatcher when she opened the Nissan factory in September 1986, although Roland Boyes, the Labour MP for the Houghton and Washington constituency where the plant is located, boycotted the opening ceremony,
arguing that the unprecedented high level of unemployment in the area was significantly the government's responsibility. He welcomed the provision of new jobs
in an area which had seen annual and often savage increases in unemployment
throughout the years of Mrs Thatcher's Conservative governments. However,
his was a relatively lone voice in adding that the Northern Region had the highest
level of unemployment in mainland Britain, and the North-East in particular
had lost 'many thousands more jobs through pit closures, the run down of the
shipbuilding industry, and the closure of building companies' (*Sunderland and
Washington Times*, 11 September 1986).

For the most part local power-brokers ignored the issues raised by Boyes and a
small minority of others, and a consensus began to show itself as the local media
was carried away by its own enthusiasm with headlines such as 'Far East Rescues
North East', 'The Dawn of a Better Future', and 'The Sun Has Risen over
Sunderland'. It was not just the novelty, but also the scale of the Nissan investment

which captured popular local and regional support and, albeit temporarily, blurred the analysis of what was happening and why. However, the way in which the local economy and its political leaders responded to the Nissan investment is important for considering the real benefits to the local economy and asking the central questions: are these benefits proving to be as great as they were claimed; how far-reaching is the transformation in industrial attitudes on which the production systems associated with Japanese management practices are said to depend; and who is benefiting from them?

In January 1981 Norman Tebbit made an announcement to the House of Commons in his capacity as Secretary of State for Trade and Industry. The news he gave to fellow MPs was that Nissan had selected the UK for its European expansion programme and that a manufacturing plant would be built in the country subject to a feasibility study. On 24 July 1982 Nissan's own announcement seemed to put the project on hold, indicating that because of the uncertainty in the world economy and the world auto industry, the company would be postponing making a final decision. Nevertheless, after a delay of almost two years, Mr Tebbit was again in a position to bring good news to the House of Commons in the form of an agreement that the government and Nissan had signed committing the company to building its production facility on a greenfield site in one of the UK's depressed regions. Regional development and special assistance grants were to be made available, and subject to effective relationships being established with component suppliers and with its workforce, the plant would reach full production of 100 000 vehicles per annum in 1991, with 80 % local content being achieved and maintained from the middle of 1991.

Conservative support for Nissan

> Subject to a satisfactory outcome of negotiations with UK trade unions and local authorities, Nissan will proceed with the construction of a car plant on a greenfield site of substantial acreage (around 800 acres) within a Development or Special Development Area. . . . This project represents an important opportunity to create fresh investment and jobs in the motor industry. It will introduce a major, efficient new domestic customer for the UK components sector; and it represents a constructive step forward between Europe and Japan on trade and investment. For these reasons I am sure the House will join me in welcoming the Nissan project to the United Kingdom.
>
> (Extracts from the statement to the House of Commons by Norman Tebbit, Secretary of State for Trade and Industry, 1 February 1984; DTI press release)

In order to assess the implications of this agreement for the two central issues of changing industrial attitudes and improving the local economy, it is necessary to consider the extent of public subsidy to the investment, the active involvement of local state agencies and communities, and the impact of the '80% local content' formula on stimulating the local economy in particular. Before discussing these issues, a brief picture is drawn of the technical and organisational features of the Just-In-Time (JIT) approach to manufacturing. From the balance of the evidence it will be seen that Sunderland's industrial restructuring led by Nissan (and coinciding with government closure of the shipyards) is of key importance for realising the success of the new management practices so essential to JIT production. In addition, this transformation is having an economic impact on the area not dissimilar to developments in the USA described in Chapter 1, namely that employment opportunities have expanded, but that the beginning of an influx of Japanese-owned subcontracting firms lays open to question the real gains to the local economy. In all of this, the issue of the local content of Nissan's products will prove to be controversial, revealing a mixed impact on the local economy that Mr Tebbit's statement to Parliament in February 1984 did little to anticipate.

When it was first announced in March 1984, the Nissan investment in Sunderland was greater than all previous Japanese investment in the UK put together (Dicken, 1983; *The Observer*, 29 January 1984). In the six years which have followed, the number of Japanese companies investing in the North-East of England alone has risen from a handful to over three dozen. This compares with the establishment of just one Japanese company in the North-East prior to 1979. Once the Fujitso factory in County Durham is in full production, these companies will employ 8500 workers (*Labour and Economy*, July 1989). There have been isolated criticisms about the consequences of this inward investment for the existing UK auto, components and other manufacturing industries: in the Nissan case these were silenced by the prospect of nearly 4000 new jobs in the Sunderland factory. The news had to be positive for a local population more accustomed to hearing reports of company closures, escalating youth and long-term unemployment, and the run-down of nationalised industries such as coal, steel and shipbuilding historically so important to the region. The North of England's traditional manufacturing industries have been in major decline: between 1977 and 1985, some 230 000 jobs were lost from the Northern Region, including 146 000 from the manufacturing industries. In 1986 alone, there were 15 000 redundancies in traditional manufacturing industries in the Northern Region. Official unemployment figures when the Nissan investment was announced ranged from the regional one of 17%, to 25% in the Wearside travel-to-work area, and up to 60% plus in inner areas of Sunderland (Stone and Stevens, 1986; NRCA, 1987).

There was, then, in the public debate a marked contrast between the region's de-industrialisation and contracting nationalised industries, and Nissan's competitive record and its promise of new technology and high productivity. The area had a poor track record, in public relations terms, of company closures and redundancies as a result of the development of a branch plant economy during the previous three decades. It was also regarded as having a reputation as a locale of inefficient nationalised industries (Beynon *et al.*, 1986). Nissan, as a world leader, appeared to offer private sector investment on a grand scale in a manufacturing enterprise unknown in the region. All the harbingers were approving, provided that there could be no exit clause. The unspoken assumption was that the size of Nissan's commitment would surely prevent it from following in the steps of the other multinationals which had come and gone in the Northern Region in postwar years, promising much more than they left behind. Here was no branch plant activity, it was thought, but a greenfield site development accommodating an initial investment of £350m, subsequently rising to over £650m, and tying Nissan to the Sunderland area for the foreseeable future. 'New jobs equals more prosperity' became the catchphrase, and the locality and the region looked to Nissan to fulfil Mrs Thatcher's prediction of impending modernisation and economic recovery. This, after all, was a high-profile investment regularly visited by cabinet ministers and heralded both to encourage the Thatcherite economic and industrial relations project within the country, and to attract more investment of the same ilk from outside (Garrahan, 1986).

Once it became known that the Nissan car factory would be built in Sunderland, and not in either of the two other major sites considered, Shotton in Wales or Teesside in Cleveland, the local communities began actively responding. Site clearance for the factory started in July 1984, and by the time phase one was ready for occupation in December 1985 local interest in Japanese life and culture was considerable. Japanese exhibitions were organised at museums and local libraries, a local community school began Saturday morning lessons in Japanese culture for the children of employees of Japanese companies, and the Polytechnic began running introductory Japanese language courses. The media covered community events such as mass kite-flying, attracting thousands of participants. A month-long Japanese festival in Sunderland ranging from martial arts to ikebana and contemporary dance was followed by an industrial symposium in the Sunderland Civic Centre sponsored by the Japanese embassy. This upsurge of community interest was fuelled by a local media fascination with Japanese life and culture, and a number of television programmes, including one entitled 'Sayanora Pet', were made against a backcloth of regular coverage by local radio, TV and newspapers of feature stories associated with Nissan and other Japanese companies in the North-East. Almost without exception this media and community involvement has been enthusiastically supportive of the Japanese presence in the region.

The welcome given to Nissan by local communities was comprehensive, reflecting a genuine popular sympathy with and interest in cultural matters. It additionally reflected a concerted attempt by local power-brokers (regional government officials, elected local councillors, the Washington New Town Development Corporation, private sector firms, regional trade unionists and the media) to conform with Nissan's preferred public image (Crowther and Garrahan, 1988). There had always been the apprehension that Nissan might not choose to come to Sunderland, and this proved to be a powerful constraint. There were few other instances of mobile capital of any magnitude interested in opening production in the Sunderland local economy at the time. There was a tangible fear that the potentially high employment opportunities Nissan might bring could be lost to competitor localities. This fear was common to all the local authorities competing to ensure that the Nissan development would be situated in their areas; ultimately they were playing a game of 'industrial roulette' in which there could be only one winner.

There is consequently a consensus in the Sunderland area about Nissan, and it is one with all the appearance of emerging to suit the company's preferences. The result of the victory in bringing jobs to Sunderland was that a consensus had to be built in the image of Nissan's corporate philosophy and policy. (Local communities in Derbyshire have recently experienced a parallel concern with public image when dealing with the investment there by Toyota (*The Guardian*, 28 February 1989). As well as seeking the same large greenfield site, with a pool of labour organised through a single union, supported by good local communications and schools, Toyota's insistence—like Nissan's—has been on total secrecy.) And so, a multinational company with little time for organised labour and openly endorsed for its management style by Mrs Thatcher was brought to Sunderland's traditionally strong Labour setting with no open dissent.

De-industrialisation, recession and mounting unemployment in the UK from the late 1970s onwards led to a sharp decline in trade union membership. Official figures cited for the decade after 1979 show a fall from 12.2 million to 8.7 million in the membership of unions affiliated to the Trades Union Congress (Fairbrother and Waddington, 1990). As a result, trade unions were set against each other in competition for the right to organise the workforce where new investment was concerned. In this overall context, single-union and implicitly no-strike agreements became increasingly used.

> Although not new, the recent circumstances of single union agreements have led to considerable political tensions between unions thus affected. More broadly, the intensity of competition for membership during the 1980s led to the undercutting of the terms and conditions of employment as a means to secure recognition. The scramble for membership involved seeking recognition on greenfield sites, resulting in occasions when employers have recognised specific unions before a workforce has been recruited.
>
> (Fairbrother and Waddington, 1990, p. 26)

There was consequently little appetite for a public airing of the labour movement's suspicion that Nissan and the other Japanese companies following would restrict collective bargaining to a minimum until it ceased to have any meaningful industrial purpose. In the context of the increasingly high levels of local unemployment, the AEU completed a single-union agreement with Nissan. The fact that this was done before the company's employees were hired and thus without their consent became a substantial element in the apparent consensus supportive of Nissan.

The consensus about Nissan in the Sunderland area stems directly from the company's willingness to put capital and new technology into the vacuum created by industrial decline. This has been embraced and presented with sufficient enthusiasm by local voices to permit suspension of rational and critical debate. An illustration is the forecast about the 10 000 spin-off jobs from the Nissan investment made by the Chief Executive of the former Tyne and Wear County Council (*Sunderland Echo*, 28 August 1985). It was possible for these unsubstantiated claims to be made with an air of authority, failing to add that whatever the exact amount of indirect employment generated nationally by the Nissan investment there was no guarantee that the local economy would gain substantially from this. Under the Nissan consensus the possibly regressive changes in working practices and industrial relations envisaged by Nissan were set beyond question. Also ignored was the likelihood that a Japanese-owned subcontracting complex set up in the UK would radically diminish the benefits for the Sunderland local economy in particular, and the British car components industry in general. The prevailing attitude is 'Why bite the hand that feeds us?', and anyone confronting this attitude in the present economic climate risks being misunderstood and mistrusted from the beginning. The purpose of the following discussion is to move beyond such confrontation to analyse the industrial realities of the 'lean' production methods pioneered in Sunderland by Nissan. The far-reaching consequences of such methods are just being recognised in the global auto industry, and their analysis in the Sunderland case highlights the general issues being faced by management and workers alike in the UK (Womack *et al.*, 1990).

THE LIKELY IMPACT OF JAPANESE PRODUCTION SYSTEMS

Before proceeding to look at the position in Sunderland in detail, there are some technical and organisational features of integrated systems of production, along the lines of the Japanese model, which demand consideration. The idea that production is integrated or concentrated significantly in one locality is not of course new to the auto industry. Ford's Rouge River plant in Detroit achieved that to a high degree in the 1930s, but in the post-World War II era the pattern of much of the multinational auto industry has been to disperse the various steps or levels in the manufacture of the finished product among different regions and countries (Dicken, 1986, ch. 9). This often transnational component sourcing network has allowed large auto manufacturers to buy in parts from depressed regions or from less developed countries more cheaply than they could be manufactured in the economy hosting the final vehicle assembly. Thus, a typical production system in the EC might find vehicle assembly in one country, let us say Britain, with high proportions of parts imported from Spain, Belgium, other European countries, or elsewhere according to cost. This type of production system is then backed up by a component sourcing network which can be adjusted to suit the auto company's imperatives. This is to the considerable cost advantage of the truly multinational company, which can then switch lesser or greater elements in the production process from one country to another in search of economic gains. A paramount example recently was Ford of Europe's decision to move final assembly of the Sierra car (the best-selling UK car at the time) from Dagenham in Essex to Ghent in Belgium. Although parts might continue to be sourced within a particular economy, the capacity to move elements of production and/or assembly between locations enhances the company's control over the entire operation between countries. Government, unions or suppliers in any one country can fall foul of company policy in this way and be manipulated by it.

From this complex process, it is evident that several major variables are at play. First, there is the corporate business strategy that might prioritise developments in new products, or in new production processes. Thus, moving around the final assembly or acquisition of components on an international basis can be part of that strategy. Equally, a multinational company might be intent on improving its negotiating hand in industrial relations with organised labour, and so engage in a practice which is called 'whipsawing' in the USA. By threatening to shut down a production facility or install new vehicle lines or models at another of its locations, a company can attempt to force local or national union bodies into lowering their negotiating demands with regard to salaries or conditions of employment. Needless to say, for this international calculation to work, a company must be able to rely on satisfactorily controlling all of the various aspects which are involved. The complexity of the situation in which a company finds itself can, however, be a source of difficulty, as well as potentially a means of improving corporate control. For example, when Ford workers in the UK took industrial action in 1989, it was only a matter of a few weeks before Ford employees in West Germany, making sub-assemblies and other parts for the UK-based assembly lines, were laid off. In April 1990, Ford announced partial cancellation of a massive £725m engine plant at Bridgend in Wales, citing industrial stoppages at its Halewood plant near Liverpool as having caused temporary closure of assembly lines in Southampton and in Ghent, Belgium.

So, the modern auto industry's typical production system can be destabilised since industrial stoppages in one place have rapid effects elsewhere. However, the systemic benefits are so substantial that dispersal of production in this way became the industry norm for the largest companies in the USA and Western Europe. Providing disruptions can be minimised and the right calculations made about relocating production, significant business gains accrue.

Reference to the normal pattern of production system operated by modern auto companies has thus far concentrated on the US and EC motor vehicle industries. Further characteristics of these industries have led them to be bracketed as 'Fordist' by some observers. The concept of 'Fordism' has many different interpretations but only one of these is relevant here, namely the definition of a mass-manufacturing organisation utilising high-volume output of standardised products with dedicated machines and extensive stocks of spare parts to act as 'buffers' in case of shortages. Such systems of mass production are in fact highly varied, and to style them as 'Fordist' is only accurate in the general sense. However, the label usefully serves to indicate those production systems which the current highly competitive market increasingly reveals as achieving low productivity. This is highlighted by the comparison of companies having 'Fordist' features with those such as Japanese auto companies which claim to have perfected 'lean' systems of production. The latter derive their competitive edge from parsimonious use of human and material resources, with the practices of 'building in' quality, of single sourcing of components, of keeping minimal buffer stocks, and of reducing trade union influence in the workplace. Traditional US and European companies have been declared wasteful in their approach to mass production, having come to rely largely on mass output in which quality is a matter of rectifying faults discovered after manufacture, where there is multiple sourcing of components, and where trade unions have been allowed to become too influential (Tolliday and Zeitlin, 1986).

The radical challenge to the dominance of 'Fordist' production systems, which were arguably at their most advanced in the world's auto industry, has by now been well demonstrated by the success of Japanese companies in competing in Western markets. In addressing this via the study of the Nissan plant in Sunderland our objective is to distinguish the most important features making the Nissan investment a commercial and industrial success. Remaining in the debate about 'Fordism' is the nexus of issues concerning state intervention in industry and the sort of environment for capital accumulation which that intervention engenders. In this conception of 'Fordism' whole socio-political structures are open to characterisation, both in the extent to which they fit the 'Fordist' model and whether this fit changes over time allowing periodisation of a country's economic history to be specified. For example, the USA has been determined by some observers to have become the most 'Fordist' of contemporary capitalist states, but for others the UK's experience of the extensive public ownership of industry and the development of post-1945 welfare planning makes it the typically 'Fordist' society (Gramsci, 1971; Clarke, 1991). For the moment the conceptual and higher-level discussion of 'Fordism', in the sense that it equates with a distinct socio-economic and political order presupposing certain types of policy by the state, is put to one side. Here preference must instead be given to discussion of the socio-technical features of which integrated production is composed, namely management strategies (including JIT) and relations with suppliers, because it is these features at Sunderland on which depends the proposed transformation in industrial attitudes which Nissan stipulates is so crucial to the plant's commercial success.

Nissan's use of JIT operations requires that labour will be compliant, and this is essential to making a success of the integrated production system. This system relies on a company effectively stopping potential interruptions to production before they can materialise. Thus,

> Techniques to countervail or remove the risks of industrial action, whether internally or in suppliers and distributors, are also usually

implemented in association with JIT management, but they are rarely
explicitly linked to JIT in the production management texts. . . .
Rather than accept the conventional management view that management's task is to accommodate uncertainty, JIT envisages management's role as being the minimisation of uncertainty.

(Graham, 1988, p. 71)

Whether or not this emphasis marks a departure from the Taylorist position on
management's scope and resources for dealing with the impact of strikes and
stoppages on production, the important issue is that managerial control and
imperatives remain. At Nissan these are enhanced in the form in which they are
articulated. This is unambiguous, even though one means of enhancing managerial control is to bring middle and lower management into more routine contact
with the shopfloor. The analyses in Chapters 3 and 4 concentrate on the control of
the labour process which this demands and the objective of instilling new attitudes
to industrial activity in the workforce, and look in more depth at the supposed
reconstruction of labour–management relations implied in the 'Nissan Way' of
work organisation.

Nissan's experience of integrated and spatially concentrated production
systems in the Japanese economy has of course been crucial in planning the
company's major transplants in the USA and the UK. Greenfield sites are common to both Smyrna and Sunderland, but additionally and more striking is the
absence in both places of any previous substantial expertise in the auto industry.
The operation of JIT insists on short delivery times, between half an hour and two
hours, and in Japan this has led to the build-up around major auto plants of vast
complexes of supplier companies (Sheard, 1983). The production chain required
for making the modern car, van or truck is variously described as having to cope
with the bringing together of 12 000–15 000 separate parts in each vehicle. The
Japanese solution to this organisational requirement, labelled 'Toyotism' after
the successes of the largest of Japan's auto firms, concentrates as many links in the
chain as possible in one area. Thus, 'Toyota City' is the name given to the vast
sprawl of supplier companies and workers' communities that has grown up
around that company's main manufacturing plants in Japan.

However, the practice of integrating the production process by its concentration in one locality has another vital feature. This concerns the hierarchy of relationships that exists between the auto firm itself, responsible for final assembly of
the vehicle from sub-assemblies and other components, and the multiple layers of
firms supplying those components. Supplier firms fall into layers or tiers depending on the size of the workforce, technological development and specialisation,
with low-value-added work allotted to the lower levels in this hierarchy. Thus,
'First layer firms are parents to second layer firms; that is, sub-contractors
providing metal working services, dies, and small body parts, and single components like brake linings to first layer sub-contractors. In like fashion, second

layer sub-contracting firms are parents to third, third to fourth, and so on down the production chain' (Hill, 1989, p. 464). In this production system, akin to an 'extended family tree', materials and parts that make their way up the different levels are subject to quality control by the firms receiving them. The consequence is that, with heightened sourcing of components outside the final vehicle assembler, the risk of failing the quality test is passed down the hierarchical production chain from one level to the next.

By contrast, the big US and European auto firms conventionally produced many more of their components internally than did their Japanese competitors, and where they went outside to source components this frequently meant inviting tenders, dealing with many different suppliers, and having less direct control over quality. In the Japanese model single-sourcing became the convention, especially at the higher levels of the production chain; long-term contracts are signed by companies selling and buying components between the different layers of the production system. In response to Japanese competition, more and more US and EC auto firms are adopting the practices which proved so successful in Japan and are therefore reducing the number of their suppliers. While it is unlikely that the full intensity of the Japanese production system will be developed in the USA or in the UK by Japanese auto firms, it is worth remembering that the hierarchy of firms has its social and labour market implications. As Sheard (1983, p. 53) reports, Japan's own Ministry of International Trade and Investment studied this aspect and found that a Japanese auto firm could have 171 subcontractors in the highest level of the hierarchy, 4700 at the second, and 31 600 at the third. Four out of five of the 13 430 firms making components for motor vehicle production in Japan in 1978 had twenty workers or less; almost one in three employed three workers or less.

Generally speaking, the proportion of women workers employed by a firm increase the lower down the hierarchy it is placed. The result of this stratification is that employees of higher-level firms tend to be male workers with more secure conditions (the oft-remarked lifetime employment), better pay and company support for pensions and welfare benefits. Workers lower down the levels of the production hierarchy of firms form the exploited and worse-off sector (commonly assumed to be two-thirds of the total Japanese labour force), since their employment is far from secure, is often not full-time, entails lower pay and comes with few or no fringe benefits (there is no welfare state in Japan). Hill (1989, p. 465) expects that US auto companies copying this approach are causing a more stratified industrial workforce to develop, and time will tell whether the UK is on a parallel course.

Core and periphery in the Japanese auto industry

Japan's auto production chain interlinks the most highly automated engine and final vehicle assembly plants in the world with crowded backyard workshops where families turn out small stampings on foot presses 10 hours a day, six or seven days a week. Connected within one auto production system, too, are primary and secondary labour markets, oligopolistic and competitive businesses, formal and informal sectors of the economy, lifetime and short-term employment, and segregated job activities of various kinds. Abundant research attests to differences between monopoly and competitive industries, primary and secondary labour markets, formal and informal work arrangements, lifetime and temporary employment. . . .

(Hill, 1989, p. 467)

A final aspect of the automobile production complex in Japan which must be mentioned is the tie-up that typically exists between companies in Japanese industry. Whereas in the economies of the USA and the EC it is recognised that companies doing business in the same industry are subject to the market exchange mechanisms associated with gaining or losing contracts for the supply of parts, a degree of intra-company protection emerges in Japan. This is in part due to the corporate links that have become established between banks, finance houses, manufacturing and service companies, forming giant agglomerations of firms called *zaibatsu* (see Chapter 1). But it is also caused by the habit associated with single sourcing of components under long-term agreements whereby these agreements extend beyond simple contracts for the supply of components to the sharing of equity between companies doing such business. For example, a firm at one level of the production system may own equity in others below and even above it. In this way there is a tight and thus controlling integration of supplier firms into the extended family tree, which is itself dominated by the major auto firm constituting the final vehicle assembler. Cusumano (1985, ch. 4) attests to the way in which Nissan and Toyota have perfected this means of controlling the firms that are their mainstream suppliers in the level of the supply chain immediately below them.

The integrated production chain

Japanese managers solved this problem [of poor quality] by organising suppliers into groups and controlling even unaffiliated firms by dispatching executives, extending long-term contracts, buying the entire output of factories, providing loans of money or equipment, and offering technical guidance in design, accounting, cost control, production management, automation, and quality control. The true payoff came as the shifting of components manufacturing and even large portions of final assembly to outside firms with lower wage scales, reduced personnel expenses, fixed investment requirements, and inventory carrying costs.

(Cusumano, 1985, p. 377)

In short, this degree of close interrelationship between auto manufacturer and component supplier originated in the perceived need by the former to impose quality controls and cost limitations on the latter. The result was ultimately to the benefit of both, since their positions at or near the top of the production hierarchy adequately gave protection by passing on risks to firms lower down in the levels of the system. Examples of such close relations between auto manufacturer and component supplier are already becoming evident in the Nissan development in Sunderland.

THE 'NISSAN WAY' IN SUNDERLAND

In view of Nissan's intention to introduce an extensive version of its production system in the UK, the first hurdle to be overcome following the support in principle of the British government was that of obtaining the right amount of land in the best location, with local authority assistance. Government grants were restricted to depressed, mostly urban, areas where economic activity was by definition low already. A rise in economic activity in an urban setting has the predictable effect of emphasising the availability of development land. Whereas land as a resource is diminished in significance in slack times or when recession hits, the opposite occurs during periods of growth. This is exactly what has happened in the Sunderland area in the mid- to late-1980s, when expansion of retail and service industries in particular occurred. This has served to highlight subsequently how new public planning mechanisms initiated by central government are making access to development land that much easier (Byrne, 1988, 1990). When the news of Nissan's need for a large area of development land became known, the local council in Sunderland acted quickly to take advantage of the land resources it had available, or could bring on to the market with relative ease.

The Borough of Sunderland was formed by the 1972 Local Government Act and encompasses the old town of Sunderland itself, the mining villages of Houghton-le-Spring, Hetton-le-hole and Shiney Row, and the still-developing Washington New Town. As Figure 2 indicates, the old town is separated from the other urban parts of the Borough by farmland, some of it statutory 'green belt'. The land originally earmarked by the Borough to attract Nissan amounted in total to over 900 acres. Given that the area is a highly urbanised one, the packaging of so many acres for sale to a single company raised many questions. Not the least of these questions was why it was necessary to negotiate with Nissan over 900 acres of land, when the company needed approximately only one-third of that space for its own factory. The total secrecy surrounding the negotiations, going far beyond the conventional commercial confidentiality restrictions, prevented many of the questions about the development from being answered straight away. It was only some years after the event that it became possible to understand why Nissan insisted on having the option to buy a far greater amount of land than its own factory needs initially dictated.

Integral to the development contract with Nissan signed in March 1984, the Borough of Sunderland as the local planning authority accepted Nissan's stipulation that it should have options to buy a very large proportion of the land originally on offer—in fact a total of 733 acres. However, no great public issue was made of this aspect of the agreement by the local authority and the government. As far as the media reported, Nissan had purchased only 297 acres in 1984. However, in September 1987, it was revealed that Nissan had taken up an option agreed three years earlier to buy a further 436 acres, bringing the total to 733 acres. In the normal course of researching local planning applications involving industrial, commercial or residential developments in the UK the assumption is that some aspects will be confidential. In this instance, however, the dramatic size of the agreement between the local authority and a single private company was accompanied by a complete refusal to release more than the barest details. There was minimal public awareness of the extent of the land sales, the price per acre paid by Nissan, the planning/development status of the land, and its eventual disposition. Callers to the Borough's planning department (the conventional access point for inquiries about local land developments) were referred directly to the Chief Executive's office, who took overall control of this development; other departments in the local authority had little information to give out.

The parcelling together of the land for offer to Nissan required a collaborative venture between the Borough, Washington New Town Development Corporation, and the former Tyne and Wear County Council. Given that such a large tract of land was involved, there were multiple owners who had to be approached to bring the land under the control of the Borough of Sunderland. The ownership of the land prior to 1982 lay with the Northern Industrial Improvement Trust (360 acres), the Borough of Sunderland itself (229 acres), the National Coal Board (209 acres), William Leech Builders (61 acres), Tyne and Wear County Council (44 acres), Washington Development Corporation (26 acres) and various smallholdings, bringing the total to over 930 acres. The first-mentioned owner, the Northern Industrial Improvement Trust, is a registered charity, and so it was possible to ascertain revenue from its land sales in published accounts and thereby establish the price per acre paid by Nissan for the land. As the development unfolded, it became evident that Nissan was engaging in the 'onward sale' of some of the land on which it had taken up options in 1987. Ikeda-Hoover, which manufactures complete seats and headliners, bought 25 acres on the industrial estate in the summer of 1987, and Nissan/Yamato similarly purchased land there as part of its agreement to supply Nissan with small body pressings. From this point the significance of land as the key variable for promoting an integrated production system concentrated around Sunderland also became clear.

The land sold to Nissan was identified before 1984 for a mixture of purposes. Some of it was designated as statutory 'green belt' (source: Tyne and Wear Structure Plan, 1979), some as unofficial 'green belt' (i.e. neither statutorily protected, nor designated for specific future development), and the remainder was occupied by the Sunderland Airport and the North East Air Museum (source: Tyne and

Wear Greenbelt and Urban Fringe Subject Plan, 1980). All of the previous owners agreed to sell their land without the need for compulsory purchase orders, and all the of necessary revisions to the land's development status were achieved so that Nissan could be offered the land it required free from planning restrictions. The statutory and unofficial 'green belt' designations determined during lengthy public planning exercises during the 1970s and intended to prevent the merging of neighbouring urban areas into an urban sprawl were now cancelled on the spot. There is nothing untoward in practice about such events, since all local authorities in the UK wishing to attract mobile investment into their economies engage in similar land deals. However, the exceptional aspect of the Nissan/Sunderland deal is not just the size and scale of the land development concerned, rather that Nissan aimed to use onward-sales to support some of its first-layer subcontractors benefiting from setting up production close to the main plant. The inevitable consequence arising from this process was that a private company would now supplant the public authority as the effective development and planning agency for the land in question. In essence, Nissan was offered control of the largest industrial estate in the area, in the UK a role normally exercised by the local elected council.

As the development progressed the maximum leverage was applied in extracting subsidies and grants from the government, using all the available powers to support inward investment and reclamation of urban land in a state of industrial degradation. In the first instance, this involved the matter of Sunderland Airport, which was in daily use by light aircraft and was a popular venue for flying and parachuting clubs. The airport was sufficiently large for a decommissioned Vulcan bomber to land there after the Falklands War and to remain as the largest exhibit in the Air Museum. Users of the facilities most certainly regarded it as a functioning airport—albeit of a limited and provincial kind, especially when compared to the nearby Newcastle Airport's regional and international capacity. Whatever else it was, the Sunderland Airport was not derelict, and yet this became its official position when the Borough closed it in preparation for the land deal with Nissan. The government definition of derelict land provided by the Department of the Environment is of 'land so damaged by industrial or other development that it is incapable of beneficial use without treatment'. The cost of reclaiming and preparing the site so that builders could erect the Nissan factory was £1.5m, and this was met by central government grants. Sunderland was at the time in a Special Development Area, and SDAs are eligible for a 100% grant towards the cost of reclaiming derelict land. Set against the complete project development, building and equipment costs of £350m for phase one of the plant, the derelict land subsidy is a small amount. Nevertheless, it provides a pointer to further direct and indirect underwriting of the Nissan investment by the state.

There is considerable debate about the feasibility of transferring the Japanese system of integrated production *in toto* to the UK or elsewhere (see *inter alia* Sayer, 1986; Oliver and Wilkinson, 1988; Foster and Wolfson, 1989). The physical

requirement for embarking on such an exercise is the availability of land. Whatever conclusions are drawn about the relative success or otherwise of reproducing
the main features of the JIT system and the related pyramid of supplier linkages,
there is little doubt about the significance for Nissan of getting the conditions right
for the ownership and control of land in Sunderland. It is often assumed that
Nissan's choice of locality within the UK hinged on central government grants
and an accessible supply of cheap labour. Added to this must be the land factor; it
might even be judged the most important.

Figure 3 shows that the land bought by Nissan in Sunderland has been developed
in different ways. The 297 acres purchased by Nissan for its own factory adjoins a
large area to the west and south. The latter is now largely occupied by a 2.7-km
test track made operational in early 1989 for the development of new models at a
cost of £3.2m. In addition, to the west of the main site is a suppliers' area set aside
for the Nissan Industrial Estate. The acquisition of these different pieces of land
needs to be discussed separately, before proceeding to the issue of which supplier
companies enter the Industrial Estate. Of material importance to this discussion is
that the options to buy the additional 436 acres of land after the 1984 agreement
was signed had to be taken up before three years had elapsed. Furthermore, when
they were taken up the same price per acre would apply as in the original purchase. The 297 acres of land bought in 1984 went at agricultural land prices, at the
time about £1800 per acre. When the remaining 436 acres were purchased in
1987, they also went at the same price. Needless to say, in the intervening three
years the high-profile presence of a growing Nissan development had pushed land
prices in the immediate area up to £20 000 per acre. One consequence of this very
rapid escalation in the price of land was that suspicions spread locally about
insider dealing involving land developers and officers and elected members of
some local authorities: following local press reports, officers from the Northumbria
Police conducted an investigation into allegations that a number of persons
corruptly conspired to obtain planning permission to develop agricultural land
adjacent to the Nissan car plant for industrial purposes. Following the submission
of a report on the matter to the Crown Prosecution Service, it was decided that
there was insufficient evidence to proceed with prosecutions (letter to the authors
from Northumbria Police, 24 September 1990).

It should be stressed that bona fide agreements between local planning authorities and inward investors conventionally involve the supply of land, premises and
utilities at discount rates (Chandler and Lawless, 1985; Hasluck, 1987; Cooke,
1989). Local authorities in the UK thus have a long history of engaging in advance
factory building and infrastructure development to make conditions attractive for
investment. This is made all the more pressing if the authority in question is
anxious, like Sunderland, to facilitate new employment against a background of
disturbingly high levels of long-term and youth unemployment. But where the
Nissan example is again distinctive is in Nissan's intentions about the eventual
use to which the land purchased would be put, namely the phenomenon of
'onward sales'.

Given that current land prices (*c.* £20 000 per acre) compare very favourably with the original purchase price (*c.* £1800 per acre), Nissan stands to make large financial gains from any onward sales of land. However large this indirect subsidy might be—and there is sufficient space on the Industrial Estate for up to a dozen suppliers—of more value to Nissan as the final vehicle assembler in a complicated hierarchy of relationships with supplier companies is control over the disposal of the land. Nissan can decide which companies enter the estate, it can set its own terms, and it can achieve the real goal of minimising risk to its manufacturing process in the manner of the integrated production system described earlier in this chapter. The efficient and timely delivery of component parts is a key feature of the JIT system central to this production process. By having preferred supplier companies on the Industrial Estate, Nissan's chances of obtaining the production benefits of this system are heightened. Long-term or single-source contracts with suppliers of motor vehicle components are facilitated because Nissan can offer both the contract for supply of components and the land on which to build a factory. Close physical proximity is advantageous when the buyer–supplier relationship is built upon frequent deliveries at short notice (a matter of hours rather than days). In the case of Ikeda-Hoover between two and four hours' notice are given to supply seats and other trim materials synchronously so as to coincide with the car bodies as they arrive in the final assembly area of the plant. Computerised links allow this to work in practice, with the result that the large reserve stocks of supplies traditionally kept by auto manufacturers are not needed. In the Nissan method, large inventories of parts cost money and conceal quality defects, so according to Nissan's Quality Director, 'the message is stock equals money, and sleeping money costs interest' (source: paper to the European Trade and Technology Conference, Sunderland Polytechnic, September 1990). Nissan suppliers with production facilities outside the four-hour delivery time utilise warehousing facilities in the Sunderland area so that deliveries can be sequenced according to synchronous production. Of course, if very large proportions of components are manufactured elsewhere and simply warehoused in the area, this raises issues about the extent to which the local economy really benefits (an issue taken up later in this chapter).

The closeness of the link with suppliers does not end there, however. As is the case in Japan's own domestic motor vehicle industry (Sheard, 1983; Cusamano, 1985; Hill, 1989), a further aspect of the vehicle assembler's connection with a components supplier takes the form of part-merger. A specific case is that of Yamato Kogyo, a Japanese engineering firm which has a 20% stake in Nissan Yamato Engineering Ltd., shown in the Industrial Estate in Figure 3. Nissan Yamato will supply small body pressings to the Nissan factory a few hundred yards away. The remaining 80% share in this hybrid company is owned by Nissan itself, and so this essential element of shared equity from the Japanese model of integrated production based on its spatial concentration is being reproduced in Sunderland, albeit to a limited extent. Nissan sets the terms of single-sourcing contracts, owns the land most convenient for supplier companies, and takes an equity share in their operations. Any component manufacturer in typical market conditions would see merits, not the least of which is security against competition, in attaching itself to a giant multinational car firm. The demand is assured for the output of the supplier company, as long as Nissan can maintain its own market position, and so mutual self-interest would seem to be at the heart of this commercial arrangement hitherto unusual in the UK domestic car industry.

Multiple sourcing and short-term contracting have been more typical in the UK (Amin and Smith, 1990) until, that is, Nissan and other Japanese companies have demonstrated the gains to be made from a quite different set of priorities. These have principally been in maintaining high-quality supplies of component parts, and in securing deliveries at short notice. For Nissan, the importance of the relationship goes much further in that it can directly exert its influence over the supplier firm. This influence goes as far as the process of designing and developing parts which will end up in Nissan cars, and it also inevitably includes the costing of parts produced by the supplier. In Japan this is recognised as an established means by which the major vehicle assembler can pass some of the financial risks down the pyramidal hierarchy of relationships which it dominates, to the first level of subcontractors, who in turn pass these on to suppliers in lower levels of the production hierarchy. It is obviously premature to predict that these inter-company linkages will be reproduced in their entirety in Sunderland, or anywhere else in the UK or the European Community. This is especially true given that in Japan the dominance of major firms offering secure terms of employment is dependent on a dual division of the labour market into core workers with all the benefits, and those on the periphery with few if any of the rewards. We are not promoting the view that a core–periphery workforce distinction is clearly emerging in Sunderland, even though it may do in the near future. But it is evident that the pyramid of relations with supplier companies under the JIT system depends crucially on the elimination of uncertainties, and one of those uncertainties is to do with upholding standards of quality in components. The close relationships established via single-sourcing, long-term contracts and part-mergers on the Industrial Estate are Nissan's ways of responding to this. This is supplemented by the activity of Nissan's own Supplier Development Team, a small group of engineers who go into supplier companies and assist in the transfer of quality control and production techniques to meet Nissan's quality standards.

Of additional importance in Sunderland is that Nissan can rely on management styles similar to its own in supplier companies on the Industrial Estate and elsewhere. A further uncertainty which needs eliminating to sustain the JIT method of production arises with respect to industrial relations: an industrial dispute in one part of the JIT system would bring the system to a halt in its entirety as no reserve stocks of parts are kept. Nissan's way of responding to this need to have complete control of the labour process is to place emphasis on loyalty to the company as an industrial ethos rather than loyalty to the union. We return in Chapters 3 and 4 to this control of the labour process and its attendant social relations of production, but emphasise here three concluding points:

(i) that the growing Nissan Industrial Estate is in embryonic form an illustration of the power of the vehicle assembly company over the firms which join in a commercial and equity sharing partnership to supply components;

(ii) that this is a dynamic situation and until Nissan's expansion levels off it is not prudent to assert the emergence of a dual labour market;

(iii) for the same reasons to do with the still-evolving circumstances of the situation, the development of a limited Japanese-owned subcontracting complex in and around Sunderland cannot be ruled out.

With the evidence that stocks manufactured outside the region are kept in warehouses to satisfy JIT imperatives, there remain many doubts about whether Nissan will fulfil its predicted contribution to the revival of local industrial manufacturing. This final point is taken up in the next section of this chapter. However, it is important to note that when examined by region Nissan's suppliers are disproportionately represented by areas traditionally strong in the automotive industry: only 25 out of the 120 UK-based companies supplying components to Nissan are based in the North-East; 67 of the company's UK-based suppliers are situated in the Midlands and the South-East of the country (source: letter to the authors from Nissan, 17 January 1991). Of the companies supplying components from the North-East, over a third are Japanese-owned.

LOCAL ECONOMIC BENEFITS

Sunderland's local economy has benefited most obviously from the Nissan investment in the boost to employment, supported by government grants under regional policy. The government's financial backing existed for Nissan to move to one of the depressed regions; if 3500 jobs at Nissan had not been subsidised in Sunderland they would have been subsidised somewhere else. In such a straightforward calculation Sunderland undoubtedly gains. However, this matter of government grants refers back to our earlier discussion of the shared-risk element of the Nissan development, involving as it does both private capital and state subsidy. When Nissan announced its choice of the Sunderland site, government policy towards regional aid was beginning to change. Instead of automatic grants to companies investing in designated development regions and areas of the UK deemed in need of special assistance, Mrs Thatcher's government preferred a policy of discretionary awards with a much reduced national commitment to public expenditure. Even so, the first phase of Nissan's factory attracted Regional Development Grants at 22% of the £350m eligible capital costs, i.e. £77m. In addition, the government used its discretionary powers under regulations affecting Selective Financial Assistance to grant the full amount allowable towards the cost of plant and machinery, i.e. £35m.

All in all this meant that using the framework of regional policy the central government subsidy of £112m represented a considerable proportion of the £350m bill for Nissan's phase one development, and cast the Nissan investment in

Sunderland very much in the traditional role of a public/private sector shared-risk undertaking (source: Trade and Industry Committee of the House of Commons, Minutes of Evidence, 15 January 1986, p. 42).

So far, the discussion has concentrated on phase one of Nissan's development in Sunderland, showing that central government grants alone (i.e. notwithstanding the local authority support) constitute almost 30% of total costs. Subsequently, the extension to phase two of the Nissan plant brought total development costs to about £670m. Based on the known regional development grants alone of £112m for phase one, a crude cost per job calculation for the 3500 jobs to be created eventually at Nissan gives a figure of over £32 000 per job. This compares badly with around £20 000 cost per job average for other new company start-ups in the region (Robinson *et al.*, 1987). Despite Nissan being a considerable consumer of state funds, local media and political opinion have continuously portrayed the company as the donor of public goods, and not as private capital sponsored by the public exchequer.

Traditionally, regional policy acted as the main state mechanism for bringing jobs to depressed regions in the UK, and although this policy was seen to be a useful one to distribute employment more evenly in times of growth, its repeated failure was evident in times of recession. When the amount of available mobile or 'footloose' capital investment declined, so regional policy failed the test. This was because it essentially served the purpose of sharing the risk of new ventures between capital and the state, with public subsidies underwriting private invest-ment. However, when private investors took their money elsewhere, preferring not to take any risk in British industry, the effect was to leave regional policy stranded. Other criticisms of regional policy refer to the phenomenon of jobless growth, whereby government grants are used to support the modernisation of production methods—often, but not always, with a change of location to a depressed area, or between depressed areas. Here the state is assisting in the process of capital restructuring, rather than necessarily creating any net new employment, although to the recipient area there may seem to be new jobs. Economists analysing this process at a national level refer to the influence of displacement effects when counting the cost of subsidising corporate changes, namely the creation of new employment in a given locality at the cost of losing employment in another (Balchin, 1990). Traditional regional policy is further criticised on the grounds of supporting capital-intensive and not labour-intensive investment, of failing adequately to generate net new employment in areas affected by industrial restructuring, and also because of the cost to the exchequer without full evaluation of the benefits in terms of new work (Robinson *et al.*, 1987).

Regional policy in the 1980s and 1990s has been influenced increasingly by moves in the European Community to establish a single European market (Palmer, 1988; Cutler *et al.*, 1989). The financial and material support afforded inward investors into the UK economy has been accompanied by a rhetoric stressing the importance of taking the opportunities offered by the single Euro-pean market. The Thatcher governments have welcomed the economic (though not the planned political) changes coming after 1992, particularly the advantages that will accrue to the City of London and the insurance and financial sectors, which have prospered under government policies. However, the weakening of the manufacturing sector in the late 1970s and early 1980s saw the disappearance of Britain's traditional surplus in manufacturing goods, and all the signs are that British industry will be in an exposed and vulnerable position once the barriers to open trade and competition are removed in 1992. Against this background, the policy of the Thatcher governments has been virtually to eliminate Regional Development Grants, except in so far as they are required to attract in 'additional' European Community funds. Selective Financial Assistance continues at government discretion with 'a shift in emphasis from large UK companies to small firms and overseas investors' (Balchin, 1990, p. 77).

The parlous condition of Britain's manufacturing industries poses macroeconomic questions about the Thatcher administrations' policies. Britain joined the Common Market in 1973, and in the last two decades foreign imports of motor cars have risen from 5% to more than 50% of all new sales in the UK. Now, over one-third of all new cars sold in Britain every year are manufactured in other European Community countries. The start of Britain's membership of the Common Market coincided with the end of the long postwar boom, and since then the UK's economic growth rates have typically been below those of major competitors in the European Community. Britain's exports to other Community countries were valued at £2.6bn in 1970, while imports were £2.7bn, but in 1989 exports were £47bn and imports £63.5bn (*The Guardian*, 2 May 1990). Examination of the evidence about the diverse impact of these trends on British industry reveals not just that Britain's de-industrialisation is continuing, but also points to a transformation of residual industrial activity, added to by new inward investment.

> Globalisation, combined with the 1992 developments in the Common Market, threatens not only to exacerbate Britain's drift towards becoming a low-value added assembler of high-value components made elsewhere, but also to reproduce this division of labour within Britain itself in regional and local imbalances.
>
> (Costello *et al.*, 1989, p. 44)

The question is, how does the Nissan investment fit into this developing and contradictory picture of state policies towards industry, and how is the local economy benefiting?

PUBLIC SUPPORT FOR PRIVATE CAPITAL

At the same time that the Nissan development was getting volume production going in 1986 the government was sounding the death knell for nationalised shipbuilding in Sunderland using the argument that there was no demand for ships in the same sense that there was a market for cars.

> The closure of the shipyards on the river Wear in Sunderland is still in people's minds. Some saw it as a ruthless but efficient means of paving the way for greater industrial diversification of the local economy. But such thinking, while sounding dynamic, misses the point. Wearside needed the shipyards and the hi-tech expertise they possessed to take advantage of the shipbuilding upturn now evident.
>
> (*Washington Star*, 1 November 1990)

Of course, when seen in the light of the substantial financial payments to Nissan just described, there is little about this situation that could be said to be driven by free market forces or left to any enterprise initiative. The state's role in closing one industry and substantially underwriting the costs of setting up another is far too intrusive, and state intervention remains a powerful determining force in the UK economy, whatever ideologues in the Conservative Party claim to the contrary. In addition, the predicted upturn in the world demand for merchant ships of the type in which Sunderland's shipbuilders specialised further detracts from the government's position (Stone, 1988). Had market forces been decisive, the outcome for the local economy could have been qualitatively different. Indeed, on this strict criterion alone ships rather than cars might have remained as the focal point for local economic activity.

Seen purely and selfishly from the perspective of the Sunderland local economy, the Nissan investment appears as a welcome boost to economic regeneration and new employment opportunities. But coming at a time of impending restructuring in the British and European car industries, state support for a new investment on this scale posed immediate questions about the displacement effects on overall employment opportunities in the rest of the UK's motor vehicle industry. Would jobs created significantly at public expense in Sunderland be at the cost of job losses in the existing, and at the time nationalised, domestic car firm Austin Rover, later to become Rover Cars and to be sold to British Aerospace? What was the national policy framework which justified public expenditure on a new foreign competitor for Austin Rover and the other major auto manufacturers (Ford, General Motors and Peugot-Talbot), which had all been in receipt of public subsidy of one form or another in the past? The answer, as time has shown, lies in the government's determination to offload Rover on to the private sector, whatever the cost, and open up the auto industry to the sort of internal competition which Japanese transplants in the UK are bound to induce (Williams *et al.*, 1987a).

An inescapable conclusion about this state policy is that it is not driven solely by the philosophical commitment to an enterprise culture based on the unleashing of market forces, since Nissan is also a heavily state-supported investment. Critics of this view might say that while this would be true of Nissan, the subsequent Toyota investment in Derby has proceeded without the British government meeting a weighty part of the bill. But the point which must not be missed is that Nissan was the first of the big Japanese auto firms to access the EC market in such a radical fashion. Setting up local production in the UK brings with it the need for a capital outlay of over £600m. What the British government has done is to smooth the path of the first of the Japanese auto firms setting up operations on a major greenfield site as a means of signalling to the others that the arrangement can work. Japanese auto firms investing in the UK routinely mention the importance of the English language, already crucial to doing business in the US market, or the confidence already shown by British customers in buying imported Japanese goods. Such justifications seem far short of the fundamentally important issue to do with the demands of successfully running an integrated and 'lean' production system. Since these demands are integral to the success of this production system in Japan, there can be little doubt that readily available land, a plentiful supply of cheap semi-skilled labour, a marginalised and subjugated labour movement, and tightly controlled relations with suppliers remain vital in both the US and EC markets.

There is little exaggeration in the claim that a company-directed consensus exists surrounding the Nissan development (Crowther and Garrahan, 1988, p. 7). The anxiety to secure the investment clouded the subsequent local discussion about the benefits of the development to the local economy. The consensus of opinion is in many senses an imposed one, since the price paid for bringing work for so many to an area of high unemployment is that the matter of Nissan's accountability as a recipient of public subsidy is never on the agenda. Instead, a consensus was formed in an historically strong Labour locality that employment creation by a dynamic multinational car manufacturer is all that counts, while a Nelson's eye is turned to the de-unionisation of the workforce. This is a controversial matter which has come up repeatedly in our interviews, not just with Nissan employees but also with the employees of other Japanese firms in the area which have broadly similar approaches to industrial relations.

Evidence for Nissan's dominance over the information flow regarding its development and impact on the local economy is not hard to find. At the outset, the agreement signed in 1984 with the Department of Trade and Industry was for a two-stage project. The first step would employ under 500 workers to produce 24 000 cars per annum from kits imported from Japan (hence the local denigration of 'the screwdriver factory'). In the second stage, employment would grow to in excess of 3000 persons and production to 100 000 cars per annum, with manufacturing as opposed to assembly from kits. As late as March 1986, the official position was that the main objective of the development was to secure the production target of 100 000 cars per annum (source: *Hansard*, 10 March 1986, written answers to questions for the Secretary of State for Trade and Industry, columns 351–352). The reluctance on the part of the company and of the government to acknowledge what is now known to have been the long-term development plan to produce up to a quarter of a million vehicles per annum (with a potential capacity of half a million) stems from Nissan's obsession with keeping strict control of information about its corporate activities.

Of course, objectively the first stage in the development made no commercial sense without the second following on automatically. The company public relations line, however, was that the progress to phase two was far from immediate, and that it depended on workforce cooperation and satisfactory supply of quality components. In fact, the choice of a high-unemployment area was made with a cooperative or pliable workforce in mind, and this is regarded as a feature of most Japanese investment into the region (Hudson, 1989). The union chosen for the single-union deal was the AEU, and the agreement signed with the company was effective in marginalising union activity, as we shall see later. So, the structures of compliance were in place before recruitment of the workforce began, although it remained a substantial preoccupation of the company's selection and training programmes. Therefore, employee access to collective forms of representation independent of the company is circumscribed. Access to high-quality components was, and remains, a more pressing concern for the organisation of the Nissan manufacturing system, but as has been argued above this was also well in hand in view of the land deals. The public relations presentation of a company anxiously awaiting the outcome of early experience under phase one before proceeding to phase two is therefore at odds with some of the evidence.

Although the agreement bringing Nissan to Sunderland emerged in 1984, the company had made its intentions of building a plant within the EC known in 1981 and had appeared to stall the project from July 1982. There was then a gap of almost two years before the project re-emerged as a serious one in 1984, at which point the company announced its interest in the UK and the game of industrial roulette began between local authorities. An important question is why the whole issue seemed to go off the boil between 1982 and 1984. While the answer is a complex one in the context of world recession and can only be divined by supposition about Nissan's corporate domestic and international affairs, it does seem to reflect anxiety from within the company in Japan about the desirability of exporting capital. This could have had some bearing on the slow and judicious way in which information was released about the upgrading of the Sunderland factory's intended capacity. That is to say, the message had to be clear to Nissan's corporate interests in Japan that no unnecessary risks were being taken, and that the door was always being kept open for a withdrawal should the conditions in Sunderland prove unexpectedly unsuitable even after so many firm assurances by the British government, local authorities and trade unions.

In addition, the changes that were announced about the capacity of the Sunderland plant conform to the Nissan corporate public relations image: this has naturally sought to present Nissan as the provider of work for the local unemployed, and not as the consumer of public subsidy or as the multinational extractor of surplus capital for re-export to the home base in Japan. Nissan has put great effort into being seen as putting the local workforce and the components industry to the test, finding them acceptable, and in carefully timed stages declaring company confidence in the development by announcing the upgrading of the investment and consequent increase in the factory's capacity. This has had the intended beneficial effect of attracting a continuous stream of favourable publicity. One of the early company concerns was about market image, complicated by the discarded Datsun label, and such free and complementary publicity was an essential resource for the company, both in the UK and in Japan.

The earliest local sign that the factory's intended annual output differed from Nissan's public version is in the introduction to the 20th annual report of the Washington Development Corporation, published in March 1984, where the Chairman of the Corporation wrote about Nissan's 'third phase, in which output will rise to 200,000 cars per annum'. The Development Corporation had just been instrumental in securing the Nissan deal for the Borough of Sunderland, and had indeed acted as front-line negotiator with the company on behalf of both the Borough and the former Tyne and Wear County Council. Nissan eventually confirmed in a blaze of publicity that this was the revised target, and later announced (once again in the full glare of the media spotlight) that the revised target would be reached far ahead of schedule.

The risk for the local economy

> Because Japanese style production techniques demand a very close working relationship between core producer and supplier, often as the only purchaser, this can have a serious debilitating effect on the general industrial infrastructure. While small subcontractors may acquire expertise in limited areas of technology and quality control, they will not develop the kind of all-round marketing and design skills of the more traditional type, and within the new relationship they will tend to be much more vulnerable to contraction or closure by the core producer. For this reason, the sources of autonomous industrial growth within the indigenous economy are likely to be significantly weakened.
>
> (Foster and Wolfson, 1989, p. 59)

When the Nissan development first became known, several principal advantages to the local economy were highlighted. The first related to the positive impact in terms of the supply of components, goods and services by local firms to Nissan. So, what was the experience as opposed to the rhetoric? After the first year of operation, Nissan's Director of Purchasing and Production Control announced that only two unexpected features had been encountered, of which one was 'the faster enrolment of local components suppliers' (source: Nissan press release and information pack, 1988). Drawing from Nissan's own published evidence, the first year of phase one of the development actually saw an increase from 27 to 58 'UK-based' suppliers. Surprisingly, given the unabashed claims to be generating local economic growth, on closer examination only two of these UK-based suppliers proved to be local in the sense of being from the Borough of

Sunderland; and only six out of 58 came from the whole Northern Region of the UK.

The Nissan development was urged on the communities of the North-East precisely in terms of the benefits to the area's economy, but the agreement with the British government that Nissan cars would achieve 80% local content is misleading. The commonsense definition and understanding of 'local' has no relevance in this discussion, because the interpretation placed on it is 'from any of the member states of the European Community'. Even within that interpretation, confusion exists over definitions and in one case it was argued,

> Almost 50% of local content could be covered if Nissan cars were assembled totally from Japanese parts—the assembly work covers nearly 48% of the cars' cost. Advertising, packaging, and sales can also be included under 'local' content before a single British component is within banging distance of the car.
>
> (*The Guardian*, 1 February 1984)

The problem lies in estimating the value of the car minus the costs of delivery when sold to the dealer, but including the costs of all parts and labour, as well as profits. Thus,

> While there may be no dispute over where these costs are incurred, the point is that this measurement system allows companies the opportunity to include as many indirect costs as possible, to boost local content to the required level, and thereby avoid the obligation of buying high value-added components like engines on a local basis.
>
> (*Financial Times*, 7 March 1989)

When it reaches full development, the Nissan plant in Sunderland will have the capacity to manufacture most of its major parts, even to the point of having a foundry for casting engine blocks. But the issue remains contentious, since even under these conditions and with the agreed 80% 'local' content, the benefit to the North-East in general and Sunderland in particular is unclear. This is not about the evident job creation resulting from the investment, but it does serve to question the benefit to the local economy assessed in other ways. For there to be the growth trajectory confidently predicted as the outcome of Nissan's choice of Sunderland, more evidence would be needed of full economic regeneration, with investment across the whole range of low- and high-value-added activities, thus producing substantial technological advances. There would have to be more signs of extensive retraining and the emergence of high-skill-based employment needs within local industry. Recent research into these aspects of economic development and the comparative disadvantage still suffered by the North-East justifies different conclusions (Robinson, 1990). In the absence of any evidence for a sustained economic recovery in the area, the more pessimistic conclusion is that whatever new skills Nissan has introduced tend to be specific to the company's vehicle assembly operations, and that the local and regional economies remain very much part of a branch plant economy.

The growth potential of the Nissan plant has already been discussed. However, mention must be made of the increasing environmental pressure on privately owned motor vehicles and the greater awareness of the contribution of public transport in reducing atmospheric pollution. Together with this factor, there is the very real possibility in view of the experience of the last two decades that the demand for motor vehicles can decline periodically. If there is to be growth in the Sunderland area for the time being tied to the Nissan factory, does this signify excessive dependency on a single major manufacturing entity? The effects could be damaging.

The issue of 'local' content thus leaves open to question the actual beneficial impact on the spatial economy in which investment occurs. Once the three major Japanese auto manufacturers are in full production in the UK in the mid-1990s, there will be occasion for a more sophisticated audit of their contribution to local economic recovery. In addition, it must be added that the whole debate about 'local' content had its origins in the defensive posture of the EC auto industry. As we indicated at the start of this book, much of the anxiety caused by foreign direct investment from Japan, as opposed to say the USA, derived from the extensive productivity lead held by Japanese companies. The insistence on high 'local' content had the intention of burdening Japanese firms with typical European costs, which would consequently reduce their commercial lead. However, such is the extent of the Japanese productivity lead that they would still potentially win 'a 10 per cent overall cost advantage even if their European local content was 100 per cent' (NCC, 1990). In view of this threat to EC auto companies, the matter of what constitutes 'local' content remains controversially unresolved among EC member states.

Two countries in particular, France and Italy, have stood out against the planned free market in motor vehicles after 1992. By arguing that the transplanting of production from Japan to the UK does not make Nissan, Toyota and Honda vehicles European within the EC's agreed definition, they question the whole export-orientated growth strategy of those companies. Nissan, for example, has earmarked half of its cars made in Sunderland for export to Europe after 1992. In March 1990 the President of Nissan used the occasion of the Geneva motor show to lambast this obstructive attitude to Japanese auto production in the EC. Whereas the UK and Germany for different reasons favour open trading in motor vehicles, France and Italy have been most prominent both in wanting to continue to restrict imports from Japan and to regard Japanese vehicles made in the EC as subject to the same import quotas. Despite the insistence that the transfer of production to the UK made Nissan's products European, the French minister for European affairs warned of a flood of Japanese cars which 'could destroy the European car industry' (*The Guardian*, 7 March 1990).

The legal basis for the continuing objection to Nissan vehicles being openly traded within the EC member states does not go back to the definition of 'local' content, since such levels are agreed on a bilateral basis between EC countries and the Japanese companies concerned. Instead, the EC emphasises the country of origin of the vehicle, determined according to where 'the last substantial manufacturing operation' was performed. The EC cannot enter into Community-wide restrictions of the kind being disputed under 'local' content definitions, since the General Agreement on Tariffs and Trade would prevent this interference in international trade (NCC, 1990, pp. 20–21). However, the insistence by the governments of some member states, such as France and Italy, that there should be restrictions is added to by the campaigns of leading European auto firms themselves. For example, the voice of the EC's market leader, Fiat, carries much weight. In October 1990 the Managing Director of Fiat Auto denounced Nissan on the grounds that a special study of the Nissan Bluebird model (now replaced by the Primera) revealed that only 20% of its parts were clearly of European production; for a further 32% the place of origin was unclear; but for the remainder it could be asserted that they were not of European origin (*Financial Times*, 13 October 1990).

An interim compromise agreement is likely to be fashioned out of this turmoil which will restrict the growth of Nissan exports to several major segments of the EC market. While the continued uncertainty until that agreement is reached poses serious dilemmas for the successful implementation of the single European market, it clearly also has major implications, even in the interim, for the impact which Nissan can continue to make on the Sunderland local economy.

Another major advantage claimed for local communities as a reason for supporting the Nissan project arose from the way in which Nissan took on a high-technology image. As one of our interviewees put it, this was a case of 'all fur coat and no knickers', since the experience of work in the Nissan plant is far from being 'hi-tech'. In fact, although there is considerable automation of assembly line tasks, Nissan's factory is far from being technologically superior to say the Metro line at Cowley, or the Peugeot-Talbot line at Coventry. The blunt fact is that the mass production of motor vehicles on a line-assembly basis is probably reaching the limits to which it can feasibly, or in commercial terms profitably, be automated. While this is an aspect of technological debate, it is the essentially unskilled or semi-skilled nature of much of the work done at the Nissan (or any other car) plant to which we draw attention. For the real gains to the Sunderland local economy and more broadly to the North-East of England in terms of pulling in 'hi-tech' investment, we have to consider the higher-order skills. Here, the requirements are most likely to be in research and design for new product development, but also there are the many professional contributions associated with large corporations, namely computing, accounting, advertising, marketing and so on. There is little evidence that any of these higher-order tasks will inject a much-needed demand for skilled and professional workers in the local economy. Given the option of situating its European Technology Centre (ETC) near the plant,

Nissan has chosen to divide it between Sunderland and Cranfield, with the emphasis very much on Cranfield. As with other multinationals of its type, Nissan preferred a high-unemployment, low-wage location for its manufacturing base, but has selected a site for the ETC in a part of the country already heavily populated with high-technology activities. The Nissan plant in Sunderland is rapidly becoming an assembly plant first and last, and not an effective magnet to pull high-tech operations into the local economy.

If these pessimistic observations about the sorts of contribution Nissan is making to the local economy in the North-East of England are valid, a sense of *déjà vu* is justified. It is less than a quarter of a century ago that the area was said to be rescuable from terminal economic decline following the dramatic closures of large parts of the Durham and Northumberland coalfields. The rescuers then were the multinational firms with footloose investment to deliver; in their sights was a willing workforce backed up by government subsidies. Then, major companies like Courtaulds, ICI and many others invested in the economy of North-East England, only to leave or sharply contract their operations when the economic depressions of the 1970s occurred (Beynon *et al.*, 1986; Hudson, 1989). Serious doubts must therefore exist about how genuine any multinational company can be, especially when it is given a free rein, in its protestations that it shares government aims of regenerating the manufacturing base of a local economy.

SETTING THE CONTEXT FOR THE TRANSFORMATION OF WORK?

Once all the direct and indirect subsidies are taken into account, the picture which emerges of the Nissan development is not of local economic revival led by a private company forging a new industrial order. Rather, it is a familiar picture of a risk-sharing venture which is very conventional by the standards of government-subsidised investment by multinational companies in the depressed regions of the UK since the end of World War II. In practice the postwar policy in Britain's declining regions was to keep economies relatively open, and to reduce the risk taken by private capital through subsidies and other inducements (Massey, 1984). While this collaboration between the state and private capital is typical of previous experience during the 1960s and early 1970s in particular, a novel feature is Nissan's requirement to approach as far as possible a situation in which the company obtained complete control over its new physical environment. While multinationals previously investing in the North-East have had their share of central government grants and local authority subsidies for land and property development and usage, none had thus far insisted on the level of control Nissan needed for it to engage in onward sales of land to its affiliates and suppliers (Hudson, 1989). It is through this ownership and control of land that Nissan has been able to begin introducing for the first time into Western Europe an integrated auto production organisation based on the Japanese model. As the analysis has shown, there is a clear hierarchy of supplier and subcontracting companies linked by more than just limited business contracts to Nissan as the dominant vehicle assembly company. Of depressing significance for the future prosperity of Sunderland is the evidence that although new jobs have been created, there is little 'net' increase overall in employment opportunities; the auto industry is providing work which for the most part is company-specific, and there is still the air of a branch plant economy about the area. From the perspective of Nissan's economic impact, the signs are that a Japanese subcontracting complex is emerging with all that implies for assessing the real winners and losers in the present period of global economic change.

We now turn to investigating the social relations essential to the efficient running of this method of organising production. There are undoubtedly human costs to this arrangement, for the most part ignored by studies explaining the efficiency of the organisational or technical features of JIT and 'lean' methods of production. The goal of 'lean' production demands there be no waste, whether of capital, human resources, or materials, or some combination of them since they are invariably interlinked. Our purpose now is to look inside the operation of this system from the workers' point of view: how valid is the criticism that the system leads to 'management by stress'; what is behind utilisation of teamworking; how flexible are Nissan employees in practice; and does the goal of 'lean' production make the experience of manufacturing work a more humane one, thus elevating the 'Nissan Way' to a higher ethical plain?

Chapter 3: **Learning, Understanding, Acceptance:**
Quality, flexibility and consensus in the making of a company ideology

It is within this system of harmony, shared values and respect for authority that the process known as consensus operates. For the westerner, consensus is perhaps one of the most difficult of Japanese concepts to grasp, particularly as it is often presented as something peculiar to the Japanese. Thus we look for something special. In fact we should really be looking at matters of degree rather than an absolute difference, for in Japan as in the West, there is a spectrum of consensus. . . . To the Japanese the decision-making process is often more important than the decision itself for often there will not be just one best solution to a problem. It is better to have a decision on which all are agreed than one which is decided by a few and then handed down to reluctant subordinates.

(Wickens, 1987, pp. 31–32)

'There are three stages in your reintegration', said O'Brien. 'There is learning, there is understanding, and there is acceptance. It is time for you to enter upon the second stage.'

(George Orwell, *Nineteen Eighty-Four*)

In this chapter we are concerned with the relationship between the roles played by quality and flexibility in the success of the company. The main question is whether this negotiated consensus is problematic. This is because the philosophy and practice of the 'Nissan Way' suggest that things cannot be organised differently.

Because of this, what concerns us is not a description of life on the line reminiscent of that genre of critical ethnography exemplified by Beynon (1984). In this case study, we have been motivated by the need to identify and then unpack those powerful ideologies that the company uses to try to ensure that the minimum of disruption occurs during the production process to safeguard continuity of work. Nissan argues that the keynotes of quality and flexibility represent the genesis of success. Indeed they are, and in this chapter we want to illustrate exactly how the company mobilises quality, flexibility and teamwork (the latter, we consider in detail in Chapter 4), and then deploys them in its virtuous paradigm of success.

It is our perception, after in-depth interviews with Nissan employees, that while the 'virtuous circle' is successful for Nissan, it represents a form of powerlessness for many workers. Success depends upon a tight nexus of subordination that can be read as control, exploitation and surveillance—the other side of quality, flexibility and teamwork. It is important to establish the reality behind definitions of new working practices. Nissan claims that the uniqueness of its organisation lies in the fact that it has broken the chains of old and discredited employment traditions and working methods and practices. It is as if invoking the idea of innovation is what matters even when the actual methods and practices at work remain broadly congruent with traditional work methods.

THE RHETORIC AND THE REALITY OF FLEXIBILITY: WHO BENEFITS AND WHY IT MATTERS

> in NMUK flexibility goes further than [occasional support of skilled by unskilled] thus, the craftsman, when he comes along, is himself multi-skilled—or at least is undertaking a training programme, which will result in genuine multi-skilling. Beyond the need to work safely, there need be no limitations on the range of tasks employees can perform, although it has to be recognised that not everyone has the same capabilities. Training programmes for the craftsman of the future have to take this requirement into account from the very start.
>
> (Wickens, 1987, p. 45)

Nevertheless, Wickens is careful to draw out the distinction between the potential for full flexibility and the reality of production processes which depend upon an imperative of continuity. He is more transparent than he appears though, swathing the potential for management control in a neutral, technicist rhetoric: '[flexibility] can be summarised as "expanding all jobs as much as possible and by developing the capabilities of all employees to the greatest extent compatible with efficiency and effectiveness"' (ibid.). This is the rub—it is precisely the tension between efficiency and effectiveness that tends to create a relatively inflexible work group. As Wickens himself says, it is not so much the work that matters, as the role of the team itself, provided one recognises that the pivotal elements in smooth working are those of power and control of the team itself. By shifting people around, you destroy the group's identity (see Chapter 4). In fact, the surprising thing is how obviously the reality of teamwork and its environment requires a greater degree of social and personal inflexibility than non-teamwork environments. In the teamwork environment, there is not much skill *per se*. If Wickens were right, that real skills (as opposed to company-specific task knowledge) were being taught, then the cost of training for skill flexibility under this regime would be quite astronomical. But if, for flexibility's sake, the training required was of low level with a limited number of relatively cognate groups of tasks, this is a different matter. We would argue that such is the case at Nissan, contrary to the implied advances in multi-skilling in the company's public relations presentations.

Nissan is quite open in its rejection of traditional notions of skill, and indeed it goes out of the way to make it clear that skill, in the company's terms, means anything but the traditional notion implied by the term. However, this does not prevent employees from accruing knowledge which could be dignified as skill. The attempt to deny control by diminishing skill begins with the debasing of the social and political content of the resource (which is what it is for workers) at the level of language. The company's reinterpretation of what, for most people, would be regarded as a reasonable definition of the concept of 'skill' is very instructive. Nissan discusses the general understanding of the concept of skills and then provides the company's own definition:

(1) What is skill?

The term 'skill' has a wide meaning and the image and interpretation of skill differs from person to person. Skill can be defined as:

- skill requiring intuition and know-how
- skill requiring long-term training
- skill as manual dexterity
- skill in operating equipment
- skill as the ability to make something quickly and correctly.

(2) How does NMUK define 'skill'?

In other words, 'to do the job correctly' . . . this is the basic concept of the skill deemed necessary to realise the original point of NMUK's activities. From this NMUK defines the term 'skill' as follows.

'The capability of always performing the operation securely, by the best operation method and the ability to further improve the method.'

The best operation method. . . . The best operation method *at present* = Standard operation.

(Nissan, 1987, p. 36; original emphasis)

The Workshop Management manual suggests that general understandings of skills constitute a somewhat anachronistic view, one that might have been appropriate in the past but is no more. Apart from 'the ability to further improve the method', the company's own definition of skill within NMUK renders 'skill' synonymous with a form of work which is really the opposite of what skill means. In place of work tasks which presume worker knowledge and determination, a definition of work is given that is partial and determined by the needs of the job at hand: in other words, task knowledge is contingent on the needs of the line and the technology—work which is reactive, rather than creative. This amounts to a twisting of the nature of the concept into its opposite. There are good reasons for this. The different definitions of skill suggested by Nissan have, above all, one important feature in common that is glaringly absent from Nissan's transmutation of the concept. They all explicitly depend upon worker determination of knowledge, discretion and control. And it is this which renders the definitions antipathetic to the 'Nissan Way' and which make the original definition of skill so dangerous. Nissan's new definition of 'skill' allows for little worker self-determination. The company replaces what are empowering notions of skill with an apparently neutral, but in practice socially subordinating, view that tells us a great deal about the relation between the work people carry out, the ways in which this work can be interpreted and the lines of social domination.

It is Nissan who will decide on each of the key determinants of power and control of the labour process: doing the job correctly . . . the best operation . . . improving upon work methods . . . the standard operation. This is achieved through processes such as *kaizen*. The importance of *kaizen* for the integrity of the 'Nissan Way' cannot be over-emphasised:

WHY WE NEED KAIZEN

Kaizen may be applied anywhere, anytime, anyplace. Our world is far from perfect and we are not going to change it overnight. But, step-by-step, we can improve that small part with which we come into contact. Whether it is at home, at work or in our social activities, the principles of *kaizen* apply. . . . As members of a team we learn how to question the way our workplace operates and how we can influence improvements to that method of operation.

(*Kaizen Leader Training Manual*, introduction)

Three groups of employees are critical in ensuring its success: company directors; managers; all staff. The steering committee of the *kaizen* team is responsible for 'Promotion and Publicity; Developing Training Programmes; Monitoring Kaizen Team Activity; Establishing the Method of Recognition' (ibid.). *Kaizen* meetings tightly police all working methods at a technical level by drumming the 'Standard Operation' procedure into everyone. Of course, Nissan determines this and the stark difference between the definitions of skill given earlier which

Nissan has helpfully provided is that they are worker determined under (1) and company determined under (2).

Flexibility is minimal. For individuals to be able to move around assembly lines for mass production on the basis of transferable skills, these skills need to be limited in their scope, for it is a requirement of the social and technical organisation of the production process that employee training will equip them for little more than low-level production imperatives. In addition, actual movement or numerical flexibility is of a limited kind. In fact, this is the trend in automotives generally, where work personnel are still central to the process of production. When it comes to the imperative of strategic integration of employee knowledge and efficiency there are really two quite contradictory patterns and considerations for management in the context of team working, allied with JIT.

On the one hand, there is the fact that even the most straightforward and mind-numbingly repetitive task requires a degree of know-how which accrues with experience. It is not just because of peculiar ideas about employee idleness or lack of ambition or imagination that workers often prefer the tedium of repetitive tasks. The fact is that practice makes not only for perfection, but for a degree of know-how about a job which, even at its most mundane, requires an element of craft to make it simpler to do and ensure it is done well. In other words, even the simplest tasks that workers latch onto ensure some element of discretion, even if it only allows an advance of time in getting the task done quickly to allow for pause. In this sense, we argue it suggests the possibility for a form of power in work. When a worker has to shift around a job, his or her general knack for the job is diminished, or becomes rusty. Indeed, the role of *kaizen* (ibid.) and the so-called 'standard operation' (Nissan, 1987, ch. 4) is one of the newest methods used by management to remove worker skill from even the simplest of tasks. So this is one imperative. At the same time, there is a need for management control of this process of the appropriation of worker knowledge. This is the second requirement. Teamwork, tied to JIT, reduces individual control over speed-ups, or for fulfilling quotas quickly for precious rest time, which the traditional Fordist managers would have understood and envied.

The trend towards teamwork and JIT is Janus faced, looking both ways at once. On the one hand, it appears to benefit employees yet on the other it helps management in the control and appropriation of their knowledge. The process is not only geared to simplifying tasks so workers can pick them up quickly, but also to ensuring that knowledge can be transferred from worker to manager to worker much more easily. The effect is to make training and adaptation simpler and therefore cheaper. But for the employer it is also a transfer of potential power-in-work to power-over-work and worker. This is fundamental in a system containing so many potential disruptions. Management want this knowledge and they seek to realise it through *kaizen* and the 'standard operation'. At the same time, what we find is precisely this requirement to keep workers on the same spot because this minimises the disruption of the team-as-family relationship (the 'doers', the 'thinkers', etc., see below). Paradoxically, this means that employee control of work is still a possibility, as is the case in traditional auto plants. Thus, the reality is quite different from the one described by Nissan, and the reaction against a typically dull and arduous workplace is represented by a relatively high labour turnover, especially in the first three months of employment.

In addition at the level of systemic integration of the technical and human factors of production, two contradictory factors are at work. On the one hand, there is the need to move people around when and where needed. On the other, coherence in production is best guaranteed by employees who understand particular operations on the line because they work in the same place on a regular basis. Therefore the ability to determine the character of skill by denying union-determined job demarcations right at the start was imperative for Nissan. However, the company's determination of job demarcations is not in itself sufficient (a) to ensure things work properly, and (b) to get people to work as directed. This goes back to the nature of JIT production processes and of flexibility, but before proceeding we examine JIT separately in relation to its coincidence with union presence.

JIT requires tight supervision of production flows and employee commitment to this. Unions can coexist with JIT and indeed much research suggests the latter can work best in a unionised environment. For example, at the NUMMI (Toyota-GM) plant at Fremont, California, the hiring of the new labour force was sanctioned by the UAW. This collaborative venture between the two leading Japanese and US auto firms witnessed the first full-scale successful implementation of JIT outside of Japan. In practice the historical configuration of forces in the local and national labour market turns out to be crucial. The important thing is not so much the presence or otherwise of unions, rather their degree of subordination to organisational codes of control and determination.

In respect of the presumed link between JIT and flexibility, the latter is extremely limited in both functional and numerical terms according to the experience of our interviewees. The reasons for this are twofold. On the one hand, inflexibility occurs as a result of the technical problems that derive from the need to have particular workers dedicated to particular kinds of line work—the longer you work in one position, the better you get. On the other hand, there is also inbuilt inflexibility due to the need to keep people in active groups organised around cognate tasks (see Chapter 4). It is from this management reality that inflexibility derives and it is one of the crucial management imperatives that defines the nature of work at Nissan. So JIT does not need flexibility, but management does. Why have teamworking, which appears to deny flexibility? To reiterate, management does not want flexibility on the employees' terms because the issue here is to do with control, and paradoxically teamworking makes this more problematic. Teamworking appears to make employees more central to corporate achievement, with the corollary of supposedly having potentially more power in the workplace. It is from this paradox of the other side of the flexibility story that the ideology of the 'Nissan Way' reveals its Achilles heel. What occurs is not worker multi-skilling, but relative inflexibility, participation without determination and involvement without control. A powerful and supporting ideological role is performed by the company's precepts and imperatives (expressed by Nissan-sponsored sports and social events).

THE QUALITY OF THE CONTROL OF EMPLOYEES AT NISSAN

The meanings attributed to and the pursuit of more quality are indeed central to the social relations of control at Nissan. As Wickens says: 'quality forms a major part of NMUK human relations policies' (Wickens, 1987, p. 63), and 'Quality— above all' (ibid., ch. 5). In defining this working environment, the working phi- losophy provides a new symbolic universe in which the employee is defined in the context of the market. The displacement of the potential that work offers of a universalistic identity based on class, for one enshrined in the principle of the market, is a crucial point of departure for the social relations of production at Nissan. It is the social relations of production for the market which the company insists is the proper place of employees in production. The worker is a consumer on the line, a consumer of his or her team-mates' products, and in turn, he or she is a producer for other workers further down the line. For quality to work, you need control of workers and hence how they have to think. We shall consider this first and then take a closer look at how quality is used in the control of employees. In the manual, *Workshop Management* (Nissan, 1987), one of the six basic principles for production is stipulated as: 'Thinking of the downstream process as a cus- tomer' (p. 4).

THE IDEOLOGY AND THE PRACTICE OF QUALITY: GETTING IT RIGHT FIRST TIME

The production activities consist of various processes which relate to coarse materials, machining, body-press, painting and assembly. Thus, there are many processes between those of your zone and the customer. Any defect in, or delayed delivery of your product would be a source of inconvenience, not only to the end buyer, but also to the downstream customers who are also your workmates. It is important that each process should fulfil its responsibilities for quality, cost and delivery time. This philosophy is encapsulated by the often quoted '"Our process quality assurance" is based on this side of the down-stream process being a customer and the quality barometer of your process' (ibid., p. 4). Just in case you worry that this 'process' can be used by Machiavellian supervisors to personalise error and harass employees, your anxiety is allayed: 'it is wrong to presume that the downstream process is finding fault with your personal abilities. You should accept critical feedback in the same spirit as it has been provided and thank the provider accordingly' (ibid.). Indeed!

How unappreciative were many of our interviewees, whose experience unfortunately does not coincide with this beneficient and paternalistic view of the supportive nature of social relations on the assembly line. After all, it is a 'market relations' Nissan seeks to define, and the laws of the market are the same as those of any other jungle. We shall return to this paternalism later, when we consider the role of the supervisory line management. Suffice for the present to note that as behind all taken-for-granted *laissez-faire* strategies is the not too distant heavy hand of the state, or in this case, company precedence, procedure and rationale, not to mention supervisor and team leader. If you accept these definitions of reality, everything will work well for you, or should, and if it does not, obviously your face does not fit.

Nissan makes clear in its recruitment material that all will not be easy working at a vehicle manufacturing plant, that it is a market environment and it is a tough line of work. This would appear to present a paradox for those outside looking in. There are the exhortations to work hard in a rewarding, but competitive, manufacturing environment, where no punches are pulled. But here at least there can be mutual respect and human dignity:

> We do not intend to mislead people about the role of manufacturing staff or the environment in which they will work. All applicants should carefully consider the following points:
>
> the pace of work will be dictated by a moving production line and will be very demanding
>
> work assignments will be carefully defined and will be repetitive
>
> protective clothing will be necessary for some jobs
>
> you may be moved onto a new operation or transferred into a different department at very short notice.
>
> (Wickens, 1987, p. 178)

The training manuals attribute great dignity to those who can prevail over what are demanding work schedules: 'it is important to develop an environment where an individual can fully exploit his [*sic*] talents in a climate of mutual respect, trust and confidence' (Nissan, 1987, p. 1). Many of our interviewees spoke highly of the 'Nissan Way', but for others on the inside looking out and experiencing the daily grind of the assembly line, the reality is different from the company's rhetoric. We shall return to this issue of company ideology in significantly more detail in Chapter 4.

The top company priority is quality and it stands for one leg of Wickens's tripod of success (Wickens, 1987). Care for the product dovetails with care for the employee and society in general. At the same time, the obvious point may be missed, even though Nissan refers to it at intervals in its training manuals, and

Wickens (1987) emphasises it with great regularity. Profitability is the bottom line for success and the starting point for further growth:

> Quality means characteristics such as performance, appearance, reliability, etc. which are attractive and satisfying to customers. The most important thing is always to strive for a level of quality which matches or exceeds that expected by the customer so that he will continue to buy Nissan cars in the future.

> (ibid., p. 2)

Wickens is more sanguine about the relative importance of human dignity and profit:

> Though employee relations might be exemplary, if the product is of poor quality, the design bad, or the market changes, the company can go out of business or the factory close. A number of companies . . . have closed their operations which despite good employee relations, have lost their market.

> (Wickens, 1987, pp. 5–6)

And if Nissan fails: 'to obtain the necessary profit [it will] be unable to survive as a manufacturer. You can see that improvement of productivity is indispensable for the company to fulfil its social responsibility' (Nissan, 1987, p. 4).

QUALITY CONTROL: COLLECTIVISM AND INDIVIDUALISM IN THE UNMAKING OF INDEPENDENT UNIONS

Quality, and one of the processes for establishing it, quality control, are provided in the manufacturing ideology that attempts to bind workers to the production process. If perceptions of fellow workers as customers, rather than as workmates or union colleagues, are created by the constitution of an image of quasi-market relations on the line, then we can say that an ideology of individualism of a different kind from that extant in other automotive plants is being generated. If people tend to view themselves as individuals rather than as members of the collective, supposedly so reminiscent of the strong labour organisation of traditional auto assembly plants, this leaves a great deal of space which might otherwise be colonised by images and practices of a collectivist kind. If workers view themselves as individuals who mobilise around collective needs and aspirations, it is difficult for a company to ensure that they aspire to a corporate identity as the dominant one. The latter is a more common ambition amongst traditional automotive producers who historically have had to battle with trade unions on what Edwards (1979) labelled the 'contested terrain'. Nissan and other contemporary greenfield site operators strive towards a fully corporate manufacturing organisation that contains within it what at best can only be described as sublimated conflict.

Traditionally, where organisational reconstruction or innovation occurs, this is mediated by representatives of the company and the trade union. It is interesting to note on this score, how different are the terms of reference which affect workers as a result of collective bargaining, in contrast to those which, in a typically paternalistic fashion, grow out of Nissan's corporatist factory regime. For all his dismissive and inaccurate portrayal of the role of unions in negotiating change in general and quality circles in particular, Wickens wrongly rejects as impractical the agreement reached between the UAW and Ford US on quality control circles. In itself, this would not be so revealing, although projecting the UAW–Ford agreement as outlandish is quite inaccurate, since the aim of the agreement is that it should cover the determination of organisational principles rather than working practices as such. Nevertheless, this is an interesting example of the way counter-definitions of how work can be organised are put out of court, either because they are perceived as unrealistic and thus unconducive to the efficient working of the manufacturing process, or are simply inimical to the company philosophy of how things should be done.

The point, however, is that to start with a new workforce without trade union power is crucial for a corporate manufacturing ideology. On this point of corporate ideology, Wickens makes great play of the fact that neither he nor Nissan are anti-union. In his history of Nissan–union relations in Japan, he overlooks how Nissan defeated the Japanese auto workers' union to press ahead with its corporate self-interest in 1953. This is an oversight in more ways than one. Not only does it obviate the need to explain why Japanese workers have been just as much trade unionist in their collectivist identities as British workers have been in theirs, but also it allows a glossing over of what the issue of trade union participation at work is really concerned with. It brings us back to the issue of the importance the company places on its corporate ideology.

Indeed, Nissan has nothing against trade unions, except where they wield influence. Wickens does not even go so far as to discuss the problems a manager would have to encounter with mutuality structures on the shop-floor, governing working practices and work methods. He betrays his fear of what workers might do if they could discuss the issues which affect them at work, in ways not commensurate with those of the company. These views do not even need to be hostile. On the contrary, the fact that they are different from Nissan's, or rather that they do not originate from Nissan, has to be guarded against. So, almost in the same breath as he ridicules the role of collective bargaining agreements forged between the UAW and Ford US, Wickens unconvincingly suggests that he would relish a positive role played by unions.

The truth is that unions get in the way of corporate strategies and create an element of uncertainty which needs to be controlled, or preferably eliminated. In this sense, there is nothing unique in this industrial relations situation. One would expect this need to eliminate uncertainty to be a main element in corporate planning and if you can begin a new manufacturing operation without unions, so much the better. What is disquieting is the pretence that this is not the case. It is a pretence because it betrays another reality inherent in the ideology of the manufacturing system itself, including the social organisation of line management and workers. It is here, in the heart of the ideological system of quality, flexibility and teamworking, that the real intent of the 'Nissan Way' is to be understood.

Productivity and profitability notwithstanding, there are more examples than Nissan's counterfactual evidence that highlight how successful automotive operations and strong trade unions can coexist. In many instances, particularly in the US, but also at Ford UK and Peugeot-Talbot, it has been the unions which have been at the forefront of considering the individual's 'mutual respect, trust and confidence'. This has been highlighted most critically at NUMMI, misleadingly portrayed by Wickens as having been saved mainly as a result of Japanese management practices. He fails to point out that not only has NUMMI survived the old Fremont GM management incompetences, but that the workforce is hand-picked from UAW members. There are other instances detailed by Parker and Slaughter (1988) where this has happened in the USA.

The real purpose of marginalising the unions in the definition games over the plant's technical organisation and the social relations of production in general is so that Nissan can ensure control. So, when the demanding pace of work which Nissan recognises in its briefing and recruitment material gets too hot for some (see above), there will be no independent space in which to define grievances except in those carefully monitored by the company. Nissan can say with all honesty and with hands on heart that it is in favour of the union (on its terms) and that Nissan wants individuals to join one. But arguably the union has no authentic role to play in any aspect of organisational life (Crowther and Garrahan, 1988). What is surprising is not that few joined the AEU in the plant's initial years (not more than 15%), but that anyone would join at all. When company spokespersons are asked about this, they throw up their hands in disingenuous perplexity and say they do all they can to encourage union membership, but people do not seem terribly interested. 'There's nothing for the union to do,' we are told, 'you see, the company council is there to provide for all employee disagreements.'

The reasons for employee apathy towards the union are obvious and it is as well to acknowledge them. It is accurate to say the union does not play a significant part in what goes on at Nissan presently because it has no really independent role, as the following letter from management to employees makes clear. The union itself is not even allowed to communicate with workers about recruitment. Employees say that these 'requests' to join the AEU often follow criticism of the company's low union membership figures.

TRADE UNIONISM THE NISSAN WAY

NISSAN MOTOR MANUFACTURING UK LIMITED

TO ALL NMUK STAFF   APRIL 1989

As you will know the level of union membership is lower than originally anticipated
—although it is now growing. We enjoy excellent relationships within Nissan and
these are greatly assisted by the formal Agreement we have with the AEU which we
know is committed to the success of both the Company and the staff. AEU representatives greatly support the Company, particularly in many external forums.
We genuinely believe that with this joint commitment to success there are considerable advantages to everyone if the membership level increases. Direct benefits
to employees include:

1   there may be times when you need representation

2   the union offers legal representation free of charge

3   the union can provide a whole range of advice to your Company Council
     negotiators

4   it can provide a comprehensive financial package arranged in conjunction
     with the Midland Bank

5   the AEU has set up a Nissan branch which means you can have direct control
     of your affairs.

We attach a membership application form and would ask that you complete this
and return it to the Personnel Department who will attend to the formalities.
Please remember that the long-term success of the Company, employees and the
Union are tied together and we would urge your assistance to make this a three way
success.

This letter was sent to all employees of the company by the Deputy Managing
Director and the Director of Personnel and Information Systems. It was hardly
any surprise that union membership levels were low, since the AEU retained
virtually no negotiating powers. The letter clarifies that such powers as the AEU
might have are secondary to the role of the Company Council which is the real
forum for 'involvement'. Half the members of the Company Council are management nominees, therefore the role of the union is dependent on patronage by the
company. There is little sense in which an independent union operates within
Nissan. The Company Council delivers participation without power, whilst the
union achieves recognition but is marginalised from participation in procedures.
The AEU has largely subordinated itself to the company's philosophy and in
Gramsci's sense, Nissan really is the hegemonic force in people's daily lives at
work. The company defines the world of those who work for it. As its Director of
Personnel says: 'He who communicates is King!' (Wickens, 1987, p. 87).

QUALITY IN THE CONTROL OF WORK: ALL QUALITY IS GOOD, BUT SOME KINDS OF QUALITY ARE MORE EQUAL THAN OTHERS

For Nissan quality means more than what the experts say, rather it means what the customer wants it to mean, although as we point out below not all customers' definitions of quality are treated quite as seriously as the promotional literature might suggest:

> The Japanese measure quality, not only in relation to the cost of repair, but also take into account the customer's perception of a fault. Thus a fault which would be discernible to the majority of customers, would be rated far worse than a fault discernible only to the expert.

> (ibid., p. 62)

Or, with slightly different sentiments but similar implications: 'Quality means characteristics such as performance, appearance, reliability, etc. which are attractive and satisfactory to customers. The most important thing is always to strive *for a level of quality which matches or exceeds that expected by the customer*' (Nissan, 1987, p. 2, emphasis in original). This idea that quality should sometimes exceed that expected by the customer is an interesting one and the expert of course is Nissan (*VES Explanation*, p. 2). VES stands for vehicle evaluation score, and is taken as a measure of the quality of the vehicle and the degree of conforming to the 'standard operation' by individual employees. In this sense, its role in employee control is very important.

Why strive for a level of quality in excess of that required by customers? Not just so that, as the manual goes on to say, people will come back to Nissan again and again (Nissan, 1987). *Which?* magazine reports of customer enthusiasm for Nissan's Bluebird do not derive from customer perception of qualities they never sought! According to *Which?* (vol. 30, 1987), pre-February 1986 (imported) used Bluebirds, while satisfactory in a number of respects, were nevertheless 'disappointing in too many to warrant serious consideration' (p. 42). The new Sunderland version was considered to be about the same standard by *What Car?* Indeed, in October 1989, *What Car?* placed the Bluebird last in five out of seven critical tests, behind rivals in its class from Volvo, Peugeot and Ford. These tests judged the Bluebird according to the following criteria:

Performance	Bluebird—last
Handling	Bluebird—last
Accommodation	Bluebird—third out of four
Safety	Bluebird—last
Living with	Bluebird—third out of four
Cost	Bluebird—last
Overall verdict	Bluebird—last

In the November 1990 edition of *What Car?*, two out of three customers considered the Bluebird's replacement, the Primera, to be worse than its rivals from Volvo, Toyota and Citroën. Finally, *What Car?* (February 1991) considered Nissan's new Sunny, imported from Japan, to be of only equal merit as compared with its Rover and Fiat rivals. The Rover 214SLi actually came top.

Thus the point needs to be made that Nissan's products are not always rated more highly than those of rival producers and in a number of critical instances actually fare worse. If our views about the quality of Nissan's products depended solely upon the company's propaganda we could be forgiven for thinking otherwise. The fact is that all manufacturers have improved on past performances in recent years. VW's commercial success over Rover today has more to do with market capacity and an ideology of superiority that continues to prevail over UK rivals, in spite of great improvements by the latter, beginning with the extensive automation of the Longbridge Metro line in the 1980s.

It should also be remembered that Nissan comes nowhere near VW in the European league of reliability and perceived excellence, and this in the context of the powerful and vociferous German auto workers' union, IG-Metall. The latter has a leading role in laying down markers for workers' positive rights in a workplace at the forefront of international technological innovation in automotives. The contrast is between VW as a European leader, and Nissan as the new arrival seeking to capitalise on every supposed advantage of a 'greenfield' start.

Hypothetically, Nissan could have followed the VW example with a strong union presence. However, this would overlook the company's chosen policy of pursuing total control. But the price Nissan has paid is the necessity of a complex and elaborate ideological social structure of teamworking, together with the ideologies and practices of quality and flexibility. The point is that the pursuit of quality is not just about giving customers a good, reliable product and giving employees honour, dignity and pride in the products of their labour. All the large manufacturers are able to make a profit, especially GM and Ford, despite being (according to Wickens) bound hand and foot by the UAW in the USA and by the TGWU in the UK. We would argue that an important reason for Nissan's interpretation of the notion of quality and the purpose behind the way it imposes this (not just in the technical aspects of line work but in the very definition of life at work) is the pursuit of control and persistent disempowerment through the measurement of individual workers' performance. Next we examine how this is achieved.

QUALITY CONTROL AS SOCIAL CONTROL

Line workers on final trim and chassis say they sometimes can hardly believe the way criticism is engendered for aspects of the finished product which neither they, nor experts and least of all the customers, would recognise. (Line workers are also customers outside the factory gate who may buy the products of other auto workers' labour, so they know what quality looks like!) For example, a closed door with a slight misalignment against a chassis is accorded a 'C-Grade fault severity' (*VES Explanation*, op. cit.) Nissan defines a fault of this nature as relatively unimportant because it does not affect 'marketability'. Nevertheless, workers are sometimes spoken to like children where faults of this nature occur. Interviews with workers at Ikeda-Hoover, Nissan's on-site supplier of seats, give many accounts of how quality, under the guise of customer interest, is used to control, rather than extend, employee discretion and dignity. For example, the amount of overlap of the carpets under the seats is supposed to have a standard character-istic, ostensibly to ensure commonality and standard working methods: even when the customer would be the last to spot it. For sure, standardisation is the result, but this hardly promotes individuality.

What does it mean to say that faults are judged according to their effect on marketability? Faults are regarded as relatively unimportant if fewer than 20% of customers would be dissatisfied (ibid., p. 2). These are people whom Nissan describes as 'expert experienced customers' (ibid.). Even Nissan describes what a customer is allowed to define as a reject product. Of course, this also admits that one group of customers are overly critical and that their perception of error does not really matter. The 'faults' in this case are left-over lengths of seat stitching which lie under the seat and are unlikely to be seen by customers and thus be perceived as a fault.

This is an interesting extension of control over and above task time and perfor-mance. In typical automotive plants, assembly line workers can 'buy' rest time by completing the task in less time than is required; in so doing they can build up small segments of time. It is difficult for employees to sustain this and where it occurs at Nissan it constitutes a problem for the JIT management system. One interviewee called Gary described this as his 'parcels of time' between completing, in this case, one welding operation and beginning the next. Reducing employees' 'parcels of time' is a crucial aspect of the control process so far as Nissan is concerned. Because these 'parcels of time' potentially allow employees to 'work up the line' (Slaughter, 1987), i.e. to build up buffers, they constitute a dimension of employee discretion. This employee rest time, like the technical aspects of the production process, needs to be controlled. To do so it is important to keep employees relatively fixed in space. This fixity, however, is usually flexible enough to extend to the teams' functional boundaries. This is achieved by assign-ing individuals to clearly defined activities within the team. In practice there can be a good deal of movement within the team, although this is often limited. In teams, each member has to perform to closely monitored task times, which makes it difficult (but not impossible) to 'work up the line'. This standardising of task time also allows employees' slackness to be highly visible (Dohse *et al.*, 1985, p. 130). If someone is not working for a few minutes their visibility serves to high-light inefficiencies in the system: thus, workers' rest or slack time is not *only* idle time from the company's viewpoint; it provides information about the production process.

Although some employees do allow their rest time to become visible, they do so at risk of highlighting their ability to work faster than the 'Standard Operation' (see below). By working to the 'Standard Operation' requirements, employees simply keep pace with company-sanctioned procedures. However, since faster time sequences are indeed possible, it is important that these are sanctioned and generalised only by the organisation so their impact on JIT can be calculated (we shall look at this below when we consider the role of *kaizen*).

Therefore, the company controls not only the task itself via standardisation, but also the off-task aspect of the performance in the run-off from one point of the production process to the next. The immediate impact is to eat into all employees' parcels of time. Management intervention here squeezes out what little discretion and time remain for workers. Nissan pursues these 'spaces' in production and employees' discretion (as in the example above, judgment in the length of carpet that could be fitted under the internal trim) all under the guise of quality standardisation, wrapped up in a rhetoric of benevolence which is supposed to mean easier, because standardised, jobs for workers. The result is pride in the job for customer and worker.

In its push for what it interprets as enhanced job satisfaction through flexibility, Nissan emphasises that even allowing for secondary task absorption of idle labour (for example, moving stock and cleaning the team area) some workers will find themselves standing around with nothing to do. If this is unavoidable, then it is better that the lack of work can be brought out into the open: 'It is important to decide what a worker should do and *let him do nothing* if he has *nothing to do*, so that at least this form of waste becomes obvious and can be quantified' (Nissan, 1987, p. 6; emphasis in original). Under no circumstances can workers be allowed to acquire time for rest or whatever else they would want to do at their own discretion. Simply put, the latter will always cut against the grain of a JIT production schedule. No one can rush or be over-keen. Discretion to fulfil norms on anyone's terms other than those defined by the production schedule are antithetical to the production philosophy and hence the company. If you do rush for a breather, you fall into the category of having nothing to do. In other words this becomes interpreted as idle time, and idle time is a wasteful 'activity'. You really cannot be too keen . . . unless, that is, your keenness is of the correct type:

> Any production volume in parts which are surplus to requirement have to be stored somewhere either where they will not impede efficiency or cause an accident. . . . Even though this usually stems from a worker's keenness in his job, it should never be overlooked when we consider total efficiency.

> (ibid.)

Parker and Slaughter (1988) define this kind of situation as part of the management-by-stress process, integral to JIT and the team concept. Although there are shortcomings with this characterisation, which we consider in Chapter 4, it is a useful notion because it highlights another aspect of the control strategy. In effect, a large measure of the responsibility for control is pushed onto the workers themselves.

CONTROL AND THE STANDARDISATION OF PRODUCTION: EMPLOYEE POWER AND DE-SKILLING AT WORK

Standardisation of production, then, produces standard-quality goods. But the process of standardisation of production, to which we referred above, is also supposed to deliver improvement in workers' knowledge and skill. In fact, it leads in a quite different direction. By skill acquisition, it is usually assumed one is referring to the appropriation of knowledge about a whole production routine. It is a long time since coach-makers performed essential tasks in the production of an automotive chassis, but their work knowledge involved skills of joinery, light engineering and painting. The conflict over the attempt to preserve the skills of these craft workers reached an important historical moment with the advent of Fordism. But of course, to speak of contemporary skill knowledge in terms of craft know-how during the early days of mass production would be misleading. This is not only because coach-makers in the auto industry were already experiencing an assault on their craft knowledge and autonomy. It would be too easy to see skill as something absolute, which is diminished and then lost, once and for all. Histori- cally, skills are fought over, but the fight is best perceived, as Thompson (1983) argues, in terms of a conflict about control.

This must surely be central even if skill is an important cultural artefact. While this is so, it would be too easy to overlook the recomposition of skill knowledge bases (though in a different form) in every new period after extant task know-how has been lost. To overlook this always seems to allow for two contradictory claims. The first is that workers are being de-skilled. This usually sits alongside the view that there was once a golden era, which leads onto the second position, namely that workers' skills are under threat. (These positions are contradictory in the sense that if workers have been de-skilled in some distant past, how can those skills be undermined today? If one argues that skills are under threat it allows for the possibility that skill can be recomposed, which is not what the de-skilling hypo- thesis allows for.) The first view seems to us untenable for it is contradicted by three moments in production: firstly, workers' claims about greater or lesser degrees of knowledge; secondly, empirical evidence for reskilling and/or the defence of skills, even in companies such as Nissan; and thirdly, the existence of management strategies aimed at acquiring worker know-how as it is continually reconstituted at every turn. In the case of Nissan, for example, this imperative is addressed by the existence of *kaizen*. Thompson is also right in emphasising that the critical issue is the relation of worker know-how to control. It would seem to us that putting the question of de-skilling this way round is more helpful than that proposed by the logic implied in the traditional de-skilling hypothesis. This is because it shifts the issue away from the ahistorical notion of craft. This is not to deny that the skills of craft workers in former times depended upon complex knowledge of production processes. What has to be recognised is that if, in social terms, the important problem was about control of work, then historically the absence of complex knowledge does not preclude the ability to control one's working environment. Knowledge is clearly a crucial element in the construction of skill but it is only one dimension of employee power on the shop-floor. As Cockburn (1983) has demonstrated, the gender dimensions of skill are of equal significance in the determination of employee empowerment.

The vital point is that even despite strong de-skilling imperatives within mass production industries, workers still acquire new skills which can and do present management with numerous headaches. *Kaizen* meetings are all about the need to continue to appropriate from workers new ways of doing the job. But on its own this cannot work, which is what the ideology of the 'Nissan Way' is all about. In other words, the constant battle to obtain the best knowledge of work routines, via the imperative of management control of knowledge and de-skilling, is not a sufficient mechanism for ensuring control of the labour process. Hence we can understand why control of work depends upon more than the retention of skill. By the same token, finding new ways of doing the job does not automatically lead to empowerment, especially in an environment where one agrees that it is one's duty to render unto Caesar that which is Caesar's. In another sense too, this point is important, because it needs to be emphasised that, Nissan's enthusiasm to the contrary, the thirst for absolute control of the production process does not necessarily make for better-quality automotive products, as their competitors with independent unions continue to demonstrate on an international basis.

Workers battle to maintain their control over many of the defining characteristics of their work and still make astonishingly high-quality products, as the TGWU and the AEU demonstrated at Ford UK, in early 1988. But for Nissan-style management strategies, any ability to pursue an element of the job that is not sanctioned by the organisation is interpreted as an outdated vestige of craft demarcation which can be of little benefit to the company. We would argue that the ability to carry out tasks with little complexity, but where workers can employ discretion, can continue to be dignified by the notion of skill, even where this continues to be degraded. However, control could still be asserted on the shop-floor and workers' skills could be enhanced, but control would be less dependent on complex craft knowledges and more on social and political power in work.

Having said this, it is still important to recognise how even low-knowledge tasks provide a constant source of insecurity for management. This is because even something as seemingly innocuous as minor discretion over small variations in task time reveals the existence of some element of workers' craft know-how. Small variations in task time allow workers to pace themselves according to the pressure of work. In a sense, this ability to pace oneself represents a form of actual control, relatively small though it may often be. Those who argue that it is not and that automotive factories are now operated, with very few exceptions, by totally de-skilled workers, should ask why Nissan places such emphasis, via *kaizen*, on the imperative that workers' ideas for production improvements should be delivered to the company, rather than coveted by employees themselves. (Improvements can mean anything from innovations in design to faster working methods.)

Doubters would recognise that employees' small 'parcels of knowledge' represent one of the main obstacles to total management control. And so long as actual living labour is involved in the production process, it will continue to be a source of potential conflict. It is in pursuit of these little parcels of knowledge that Nissan directs so much time and attention. A whole policing system exists for the sole purpose of making common knowledge what exists as a particular bit of task knowledge held by an individual, or by a group of workers. We shall see presently how this is personified in the role of supervisor. For the present, it is worth consulting the company bible on these matters, *How to Establish the Standard Operation and How to Instruct It* (*ESO*):

> [To ensure] 'better quality and cheaper products on time' . . . operation standards must be specified so that NMUK's total quality expectations can be reflected in the operations performed by each operator.
>
> The content of the standard operation should be pitched at such a level that *most* of the operators and workers can attain by education and training: and not at a level reflecting some notion of general or average ability.
>
> (p. 1)

In other words, the detailed know-how that each worker accumulates for task completion must be made accessible to those who might not otherwise be capable of doing the job as well as the incumbent. In this way, knowledge of the task is disinvested of its private, or specific skill content. This process is one of constant attrition on individual know-how. The company has an ambiguous, but inescapable, relation to worker know-how; it is at once a threat to the company, for it can lead to worker-control-in-work, but when rendered generalisable through the imperative that everything belongs to the company, it becomes a boost to the enterprise. As the *ESO* continues: 'The standard operation is the best method currently available. But a better method must be considered and established in order to secure improvement and to attain a levelling-up of the group's skill'. That is to say; the company seeks to reduce the individual worker's specific set of task knowledges, or 'parcels of knowledge' as we call them. The *kaizen* process represents the institutionalisation of this appropriation of workers' know-how, by means of an internal job evaluation process which is compulsory for all workers (although it is very rare for white-collar, especially clerical, staff to be involved in *kaizen*).

Since workers often promote product improvements and, in many cases, time savings on task cycles, they are further boosting company profits without any financial or other reward. As Wickens says: 'Because of the view that problem solving and continuous improvement are part of everyone's job we made the decision not to give any financial reward for achievement—to do so would be to make it special' (!) (Wickens, 1987, p. 71). This hardly requires a second glance for its full significance to be obvious. It suggests an enormous confidence and complacency in the strength of the 'Nissan Way' to prevail over contrary sentiments about the form that rewards might take. This could only be believed and it could only work in the way that it does if a manufacturing company were sufficiently confident that little or no opposition would arise. That this is the case is both cause and consequence of an overriding organisational imperative which is both part of, and extends, an apparatus of surveillance and control that by definition excludes the *framework* for other world views. Indeed, were this *not* Nissan's aim, so much time and financial resources would not be so committed to ensuring compliance.

To summarise then: worker know-how is continually being transferred to management through *kaizen*. In addition, the company philosophy is geared toward the expectation that workers will continue to give up their small pieces of information, or 'parcels of knowledge', so that: 'The company [can] obtain more profit, and to return a part of it to its employees and stock holders' (Nissan, 1987, p. 4). Nissan's all-persuasive system of surveillance and control of labour is exemplified most clearly in its instructions for supervisors. It is through the activities of the supervisor that the policing of the labour process can be guaranteed. Whilst line workers perform a critical role in this process, the supervisor's part is vital as the main conduit of company lore and as the tangible personality who can act to coordinate the labour process in each zone. The team leaders act as his (there are no women supervisors of line workers) subalterns, communicating information and impressions of workers up and down the hierarchy.

SUPERVISORS AT WORK: CONTROL AND SURVEILLANCE

The supervisor's role is broadly described as having two essential components: (a) 'to achieve the production target' and (b) 'to develop his team' (Nissan, 1987, p. 11). Included in these broadly defined components is the requirement to ensure 'daily workshop control' (ibid., p. 46). This 'includes the control of quality, standard operation, health and safety, cost, equipment and labour—the so-called six controls that the Supervisor must maintain for the achievement of the production goals' (ibid.). But to discover more about how this 'daily workshop control' impacts on the *social* role of supervisor, we need to consider it more closely under the rubric of (a) and (b) above, where both of these relate to the surveillance and control of labour in maintaining and increasing the rate of exploitation. (For more information concerning the routine content of a supervisor's work, see 'One Foreman's Daily Actions'; ibid., p. 50.) It is important in this respect to keep in mind what we emphasised above, namely, that the organisation works because it operates within a determinate ideological framework of consensus for subordination. In Chapter 2 of *Workshop Management* (Nissan, 1987), Nissan details five aspects of a supervisor's role which seek to sustain and extend this framework:

1   The need to establish the standard approach.
2   Subordinates need to be able to acquire and follow the standard operation.
3   Supervisors must 'research for a better procedure' (p. 15).
4   'Abnormalities' must be identified and dealt with. This is known as 'Abnormality Control'.
5   Finally, the supervisor must establish a better production environment.

It is worth considering these imperatives as they link together to provide for a system of worker surveillance, control and acquisition of knowledge for the appropriation of surplus value.

The first and second tasks represent conventional Taylorist imperatives for the acquisition of the best know-how for the task, appropriated from maintenance workers, engineers and from those elements of skill held and re-created by line workers. This is clear from the *ESO* manual:

1) What is operation analysis?

'Operation analysis' is to analyse in detail the actual sequence of one . . . operation or the editing unit operation . . .

Purpose

* When the standard operation is established, the main steps and vital points can be easily identified and extracted.
.
.
.

2) How to determine actions
.
.
.

* The action stroke is the unified factor action, which is the sum combination of small individual work factor operations.

(Factor operation)

* Extend the right hand * Pick up a screw * Insert through seal	* Take a screw in the right hand * Insert screw through the seal	Insert screw through seal with right hand

(unit of factor action)   (unit of operation analysis) (p. 25)

In addition, the supervisor has the responsibility for inculcating the company's work norms into 'subordinates' (Nissan, 1987, p. 19). By going beyond Taylorism, however, this establishes the *social* dimension for the control of workers on the line:

> Also, supervisors must not forget to teach their subordinates *why* the standard operation must be complied with and what happens if they fail to do so. . . . [T]he supervisor must develop his subordinates' will and sense of responsibility in producing a good product and supplying it to the customer.

> (ibid. p. 14)

It is then impressed upon the supervisor that there is a need to seek out and excise what is termed 'Abnormality', 'in spite of compliance with the standard operation' (ibid.).

So, 'subordinates' must be informed of the 'abnormality' and the reasons why it should be eliminated. This process is the central mechanism which on a day-to-day basis constitutes the surveillance of workers. Three out of five reasons cited for the appearance of 'abnormalities' are directly attributed to the workers themselves: 'Failure to follow the standard operation'; 'Defective parts, or the possibility of them appearing'; 'A point goes beyond a line in a process control chart' (ibid., p. 15). In other words, 'non-conformance with the standard or failure to comply with the standard are defined as abnormality' (ibid.). The point about this control is that it is geared to finding out not just whether deviations from the norm lead to impairment of quality. To recall, the view of deviation from quality, as outlined above, suggests that much of what passes for error is unimportant except for those 20% of customers who find fault. According to Nissan, these are fairly minor 'problems'.

One of the principal reasons for so much concern over deviation from the standard norm is to continue to keep track of how employees themselves do the job so that the company can maximise on minute and novel procedures for task cycles. After all, the 'Guidelines' in no way imply that deviation from standards will necessarily lead to low-quality products. Indeed, this correlation is studiously avoided. But where workers do find new ways that might improve upon existing methods, these must be institutionalised by *kaizen* meetings.

It was only after we were able to link together innovation in work methods and appropriation of worker knowledge via *kaizen*, within the overall framework of control, that we were able to account for how it was that our interviewee, John, felt discontented (see Chapter 5, p. 124). In this instance, even though an employee introduced time-saving techniques on his own initiative, he fell foul of the company's control, surveillance and appropriation strategies. It was not that he did not work hard or innovate, rather that he was not forthcoming to his supervisor sufficiently often in advance. All time-saving techniques must be justified at *kaizen* meetings before they can be adopted; it is not left to individual workers to innovate on their own—although, this does not prevent workers from sometimes coveting their own precious methods, where they can.

In an important sense, all the supervisors' tasks mesh together in the execution of control, surveillance and the appropriation of surplus value (supervisor's tasks are spelt out in *Workshop Management*, pp. 14–20; Nissan, 1987). But tasks 3 ('Research for a better procedure') and 5 ('The establishment of a better production environment') are central to pursuing worker improvements in the manufacturing cycle and in the further appropriation of surplus value: 'each supervisor must do his best to upgrade his workers' ability as well as his own and encourage the personal growth of the individual worker' (ibid., p. 12). To summarise the supervisor's role diagrammatically:

CONTROL	SURVEILLANCE	APPROPRIATION OF SURPLUS VALUE (exploitation)
Tasks: 1 & 2 (see list above, p. 78) Induction and defining nature of job	4 Checking for abnormalities ('Abnormality control')	3 & 5 Continuously searching for better methods

Quality, then, is part of the process of subordination of employees at Nissan, but it is only one aspect of the tripod of factors, and depends upon consensus for success. This second leg of the 'Nissan Way' is organisationally vital in pursuit of the coveted position of market leader.

FLEXIBILITY AND CONTROL

Previously we highlighted the relation between the company's rhetoric on flexibility and the assault on skill in general. Here we want to draw out the links between flexibility and social and ideological control. We have already pointed out that internal control is premised on a requirement to calculate out of the work process unpredictability, as determined by a JIT system. At the same time, we argued that this leads to less flexibility because of this control requirement, i.e. predictability of resource input. This impacts directly on quality, which itself requires dedicated and predictable inputs. Flexibility and quality act as mechanisms for ensuring standardisation. This in turn leads to a persistent assault on skill. In the next two sections, we want to focus on the ideology of flexibility proper and on how it ties into the 'Nissan Way'. Wickens is right in asserting that flexibility, like quality, is axiomatic to the 'Nissan Way'. It is not an optional extra but a leg of his crucial tripod, 'Flexibility, Quality, Teamwork'. But of course, this aphorism for the company's virtuous circle obscures as much as it reveals.

Flexibility, like quality and teamworking, is something everyone can agree on, or aspire to, if the climate is right. However, the company's call for flexibility obscures how it works, why it works and for whom it works. To pose these questions is to risk wondering whether there might not be different ways of interpreting who the beneficiaries of the virtuous tripod might be. The way Nissan tells it, it is a tautology: *flexibility* allows for and ensures *quality* . . . which depends upon *teamwork* . . . that promotes *quality* and therefore *teamwork* and *flexibility*. In fact, any one of these could be transposed for the other. Indeed, the intention behind Nissan's interpretation of these virtues is to try to turn them into cyphers for each other in the public consciousness. However, just as we cannot take for granted the view that quality is what Nissan says it is, so when it comes to the definition of flexibility we need to be alert for another word from the company vocabulary. Flexibility is as central to the 'virtuous circle' of control, surveillance and exploitation as is quality and teamwork.

To understand just how 'flexibility' achieves this important status at Nissan, and in Wickens' lexicon of necessary organisational virtues, it is important that we recognise how it is achieved and what role it serves in the search for employee commitment and organisational coherence. In short, what part does flexibility play in the formation and putting into operation of cycles of control, surveillance and exploitation? We have already referred to Wickens' careful description of what flexibility at work does not consist of. It is worth taking a look at what he actually says here: 'What exactly do we mean by flexibility? Certainly not moving people rapidly from section to section for that detracts from teamworking' (Wickens, 1987, p. 44). He then offers this by no means anodyne interpretation: flexibility means 'expanding all jobs as much as possible and developing the capabilities of all employees to the greatest extent *compatible with efficiency and effectiveness*' (ibid.).

The company seeks to achieve this by distinguishing tasks using just two jobs titles: 'Manufacturing Staff' and 'Technicians'. There are supposed to be no barriers to employees' ultimately being able to carry out all tasks falling within the remit of these two broad job designations. However, as we mentioned previously, there is one crucial obstacle to flexibility, as the quotation from Wickens makes clear. Teamwork, which is vital in constituting and mediating the determinate social relations of domination in the plant, plays a significant role in limiting the scope of flexibility (see Chapter 4). Nissan is supported in what it describes as the expansion of the range of workers' skills by the agreement with the AEU. It was this agreement which was supposed to provide the 'bedrock' for success:

(a) To ensure the fullest use of facilities and manpower, there will be complete flexibility and mobility of employees.

(b) It is agreed that changes in technology, processes and practices will be introduced and that such changes will affect both productivity and manning levels.

(c) To ensure such flexibility and change, employees will undertake and/or undertake training for all work as required by the Company. All employees will train other employees as required.

(NMUK, 1985)

Taking this alongside Wickens's advisedly cautious note about what flexibility does not mean, we gain a clearer insight into what it can involve. The point is that the movement of labour around the plant can occur, but the real issues are about the 'who' and the 'how' of the determination of flexibility. Flexibility is linked with the major problem of the control and determination of the allocation of labour. This is hardly a great secret, as both Nissan and the AEU admit. But it is problematical once we go beyond the taken-for-granted benefits this system offers Nissan workers themselves.

Just how much they benefit can only be judged in a context which recognises how much they actually lose. It will be useful at this point if we unpack the simplifications and the obviousness of the supposed benefits of flexibility. What these supposed benefits obscure are the real disadvantages of Nissan's code of flexibility. That these 'benefits' are in fact precisely the opposite of what they claim to be and that they reinforce the diminution of skill is central to our argument. Nissan's defence of the strengths of its form of flexibility depends on an ideology of mutual benefit and personal development. However, this system supports a form of working which in fact contains all the defects and prejudice the company attributes to the supporters of the supposedly outworn imperatives of craft demarcation. We shall consider these each in their turn in a moment. In general terms, flexibility for Nissan is about those management imperatives that define time allocation for job tasks, movement of labour and, again, that vital element of subordination, employee participation in quality control. We can say that flexibility has at least three dimensions in Nissan's overall regime of control, surveillance and exploitation:

1   Raised level of skill.
2   Mutual support and trust because of, and in turn supportive of, 1.
3   Better quality because everyone is aware of the overall nature of the production process.

All of these appear as reasonable because they cover both the employee's needs, 1 and 2, and those of the company and the customer, 3. In fact, although the company keeps rather vague the possibility of what the new skills acquired will consist of, it allows for the possibility that the new flexible worker's skills could consist of anything. If this is tied to a popular definition of skill then it can obviously be made to look attractive. However, the only really new craft tasks which could in any sense be so described are those of quality control. And here, one is very quickly back to surveillance; to the processes of Neighbour Check,

Vehicle Evaluation System (VES) and *kaizen*. The importance of these in the process of self-subordination and their relative impact on different groups of workers in different ways and at various times will be discussed in the next chapter.

For Nissan, operationalising the surveillance processes is critical in the assault on old and 'outdated' notions of skill. In general terms, the organisation perceives that this requires a necessary and general erosion of the distinction between skilled maintenance workers, semi-skilled line workers and unskilled line workers, with the general aim of developing multi-ability skilled workers. In practice, what we found is the creation of company-specific skills by workers performing only a limited range of cognate tasks. These tasks tend to be limited in their range of utilisation and also in the degree of variation in their spatial location throughout the company. According to Terry, who works in the paint shop, both functional and numerical flexibility are really quite limited:

Terry: On-line I would say I move around pretty rarely. On-line you are given a specific job to do and it is very rare you will change from that job unless somebody is absent and you have got to cover. So obviously where I work now I have been on-line and I know most of the jobs on-line. So there is usually like a floater type thing, a cover for people, but if you have more than one person off, say like two or three, where I work I can do anything in my section.

Q: Even though the jobs might be different?

Terry: Even though they are quite different, yeah.

Q: Would you work within one team?

Terry: Yeah. You'd stick within the one team in the one zone. I have known it, say a few times, if there were a shortage of people—say you are struggling to meet a target—they have brought in somebody from another zone which is similar to help you out. But that is as far as it will go like. They would not bring in somebody from a totally different zone.

Therefore, the company's pursuit of flexibility leads to a reduction in actual discretion and control, the main determinants of skill and long-term satisfaction at work. The icons of quality and flexibility (or, to put it in a fashion rather more in keeping with the company's ideological imperatives—flexibility for quality), in its overall aim of establishing authority at work, lead to a general diminution of employee autonomy and empowerment. If actual skill enhancement was occurring, one would expect to see these two indices enhanced.

The three dimensions of flexibility can be looked at again (Table 1), but this time in the light of our proposition about the relation between skill and empowerment:

Table 1

FOR NISSAN FLEXIBILITY MEANS:	REALITY OF FLEXIBILITY AT NISSAN:
1. Enhanced skill	1. Skill is diminished
2. Mutual trust and support between employees and company due to 1	2. More tasks but less control—this is linked to command and integration system
3. Better quality is believed to derive from 1 and 2	3. This claim cannot be made unless the relationship between the mechanisms used in the pursuit of quality are properly related to the role these play in control and exploitation of labour

THE IDEOLOGY OF CRAFT AND FLEXIBILITY IN THE TRIPOD OF SUCCESS

The tripod represents the substance of Nissan's claims about the importance and attraction of flexibility. Certainly, management have it all their own way here and they believe they are onto a winner when they claim that the upgrading of skills is what Nissan's form of flexibility is all about. Nissan will apparently create multi-skilled employees with better career prospects than the old craft approach would allow for. The quotation from Wickens (1987, p. 44) has already interestingly shown how a broad range of tasks necessarily passes for multi-skilling. Further to this, Wickens argues that those training programmes 'which still retain the single craft approach are preparing young people for a limited career' (Wickens, 1987, p. 45). Suffice to say that this is precisely what Nissan itself creates—skills which are only of practical value inside the organisation. It is not the case that generalised multi-skilling occurs. From our interviews, it is clear that many ex-engineers and fitters, whose skills are still in demand outside Nissan, found that what passed for multi-skilling was really knowledge of a number of general and cognate tasks. These are almost entirely company specific.

What really occurs at Nissan, in terms of employee know-how, is not a situation that leads to job enhancement, but rather a series of social and technical organisational processes that ensures worker disempowerment. These can be summarised as:

1   *Job enlargement.* What this involves is a process in which cognate manual skills covering different movements are acquired by workers. In no normal sense of the word can this be described as multi-skilling (as Nissan describes it). What does occur is a process of job enlargement and this tends to be vertically downward. A good instance of this would be where technicians take on 'indirect' (preparation) tasks when setting

up the line, or cleaning-up the zone after work finishes. This multi-functionality ensures the steady accretion of tasks.

2   *Task accretion* guarantees work intensity (Pollert, 1988a; Elger, 1989). This ensures that where obstacles to production might occur as a result of staffing difficulties within and between different teams and zones (although there is little movement in practice between either), de-skilled work allows for the imperative of resource allocation to be quickly resolved. In practice, this is usually about workers covering for one another where they are performing cognate tasks within the same team, or in cognate teams. This is a vital requirement at Nissan, because JIT demands the speedy distribution of resources throughout the company if organisational and production continuity is to be guaranteed. This task accretion leads to work intensification.

3   *Intensification of effort in work.* This depends on a squeezing out of worker discretion of idle time. The process is helped by the fact that task cycles within teams require a principle of no standard-task-time so that innovations in working methods and practices accrued from *kaizen* can be used to alter the rhythm and tempo of effort when deemed necessary. *Kaizen*, then, ensures that in effect, employees work towards lower time sequences for tasks. Where *kaizen* is about 'quality', it is also a quality-and-effort principle whereby intensified work can be assessed for the effect that it has on the outcome of production. Thus, *kaizen* is also a means for transferring problems in product quality onto workers. This is supported by the system of worker peer surveillance, the 'Neighbour Check' code, which involves colleagues assessing one another's 'quality' and performance. This substitutes workers for supervisors in maintaining discipline (Garrahan and Stewart, 1989, 1991b). 'Quality' problems are correspondingly interpreted as arising out of individual confusion or a lag in 'skill', as Nissan would call it, during line speed-ups. This brings us to the importance of extra-technical forms of subordination.

4   *Subordination which is based on non-technical factors.* These derive from the 'Nissan Way' (see also Garrahan and Stewart, 1992). *Kaizen* and team-working are vital to the manufacture of consent for subordination in the organisation. These constitute the new regime of subordination.

In Nissan, employee autonomy, up-skilling and knowledge enhancement are important elements in managerial strategies and the way they link to new manufacturing techniques. Subordination at work is enhanced by the particular form of association in the work organisation and it is characterised by the four features above, which are indices not of employee empowerment but of enhancement of employer power and control.

Nissan's view is that multi-skilling (a term the company hopes implies the notion of 'up-skilling') is what its training strategy is concerned with. This view can only really be maintained in an employment environment where the kind of world described by the 'old' and outdated terms ceases to have any meaning. This is because in the new environment the circumstances and factors that gave rise to the 'old' terms cease to mean, for those with memory, what they once did.

There are a number of entirely understandable reasons why this state of affairs should continue to grow at such a pace. By a cruel blow, caused by the historical failure of the collective power of labour, the old terms and concepts are being turned into their opposites. Collective memory is crucial in the battle to defend those very forms of worker empowerment enshrined in the struggles (otherwise defined as the collective resources for defence of continuity and control) of previous generations of craft and skilled workers. The notion of struggle as central to what we understand by craft is significant here, because struggle is a major determinant in the retention of skill and craft. This is still the case; employees at Nissan continue to come up with better working methods (as we pointed out above), which they occasionally hold as sacrosanct.

In Marquez's parable of, among other things, the perils that befall the end of collective memory, the inhabitants of Macondo only remember what to do with objects, animate and inanimate, by sticking on little annotations each day, describing the character and function of everything afresh. Without these 'names' and instructions, there can be no nemesis for those who deceive, because when people forget what things mean, other deceivers can step in to reinforce the process. This is one way in which individual and collective power can be lost. The loss is inevitable when the power to define the real is given over to other people, or is usurped, because when power is lost so is control, according to any traditionally conceived collective definition of the word. 'Thus they went on living in a reality that was slipping away, momentarily captured by words, but which would escape irremediably when they forgot the value of the written words' (Gabriel García Marquez, *One Hundred Years of Solitude*).

To be able to espouse a particular view of the world—without challenge— suggests that an extremely sophisticated organisational environment is being regularly reproduced. For this to work, there needs to be at least two dependable variables: a strong corporate ideology (we have seen already something of how this ideology operates with respect to quality and flexibility) and a secure and virtuous social environment. This is where teamworking—the third leg of the Nissan tripod—comes in, and it is to this that we now turn. Teamworking is the most important variable in the 'virtuous' circle for it provides for the social basis of, and thus the coherence for, the 'Nissan Way'.

Chapter 4: **Teamworking and the Social Organisation of Control**
He who communicates is king (Wickens, 1987)

TEAMWORK AND 'MANAGEMENT-BY-STRESS'

Teamworking and the philosophy known as the team concept are an accepted part of most management strategies in Japanese automotive companies and occupy the pivotal role for many others internationally. Teamwork strategies are particularly advanced in the USA and have provided the organisational and social philosophy for the much-praised Toyota-General Motors plant at Fremont (NUMMI). It is also vital at the Chrysler-Mitsubishi (Diamond-Star) complex at Normal, Illinois, and the starting point for the long-awaited GM 'new age' operation, known as 'Saturn', in Tennessee (close to Nissan's Smyrna operation), which began production in the summer of 1990.

Most of the research in the USA on the social and political impact of teamworking on unions and workers in general, has been carried out by a labour movement group organised around the bulletin *Labour Notes*. The most widely available work by contributors to *Labour Notes* is that of Mike Parker and Jane Slaughter (1988, 1989). Parker and Slaughter's argument centres on the place of teamwork within an overall management package, which they describe as management-by-stress. We shall come to this presently, but for the moment, we consider what they see as the lure which teamwork holds for organisations and employees respectively, and their view that teamwork, as operated by management, is just another trick to get workers to work harder by giving them less space to object (via management-by-stress) and by eliciting their consent.

Components of teamworking

1. A rewritten contract announcing that a new relationship exists between the company and its workforce.

2. Interchangeability, meaning that workers are required or induced (through pay-for-knowledge) to be capable of doing several jobs.

3. Drastic reduction of classifications, giving management increased control to assign workers as it sees fit. The abolition of classifications and interchangeability in job assignments are the main things management wants when it talks about team concept.

4. Less meaning for seniority. In some cases seniority is explicitly undermined or modified. In other cases, opportunities for exercising seniority disappear. For example, if classifications are eliminated, opportunities to transfer to different classifications by seniority are also eliminated.

5. Detailed definition of every job step, increasing management control over the way jobs are done.

6. Workers' participation in increasing their own workload.

7. More worker responsibility, without more authority, for jobs previously performed by supervision.

8. A management attempt to make workers aware of the interrelatedness of the plant's departments and the place of the individual in the whole; an attempt by union and management to get away from the 'I just come to work, do my job and mind my own business' outlook.

9. An ideological atmosphere that stresses competition between plants and workers' responsibility for winning work away from other plants.

10. A shift towards enterprise unionism, where the union sees itself as a partner of management.

(Parker and Slaughter, 1988, p. 5)

Parker and Slaughter further argue that teamworking appeals to workers because 'Through teamwork—everyone pulling together—we can increase productivity, improve quality, enhance job satisfaction and save jobs. Even allowing for some hype it seems too good not to try' (Parker and Slaughter, 1988, p. 4).

This 'package is really a means by which management uses workers' fondly held collective work experiences for the company's own ends; however, management claims that it will ultimately help workers to strive for dignity. In other words, according to Parker and Slaughter, teamwork as management tell it can be something of a sham.

What's in a team?

The team concept starts with the assumption that workers must be interchangeable. Management says that teamwork requires getting rid of classifications and that all team members must learn all the jobs on the team.

This use of the work 'team' is special and peculiar. Management uses the word because of its positive associations from other areas of life: sports teams, surgical teams, management teams, union leadership teams, and so on.

But in every one of these cases, 'team-work' implies the cooperation of specialists towards a common goal. The qualities that make a good wide receiver in football are not the same as those of a centre. The neurosurgeon and the anesthesiologist cannot substitute for one another. . . . Rarely is one person exceptional in all areas.

In fact, the main place in our language where 'team' implies interchangeable members is where it refers to a team of horses—beasts of burden of equal capabilities, yoked together to pull for a common end (determined by the person holding the whip).

(ibid., p. 4)

Even where teamwork operates apparently in the interests of the workforce, it centres on intensification in the rate of exploitation through increasing social and organisational measures which heighten management control. It is the very notion of a team which, appealing to workers' class experience of collective effort and community experience of solidarity, can be used to 'con' workers into accepting what is mostly old wine in new bottles.

There are bound to be differences from traditional arrangements in the organisation of labour where companies utilise teamworking. However, teamwork is carried out through the integrated package which Parker and Slaughter describe as management-by-stress. As we point out below, one of the features of management-by-stress (at Nissan, it may be understood as only one of the important features of teamworking proper) is that because it entirely colonises all sociospatial locations within the factory, the scope for collective oppositional activity is reduced to a minimum. However, this does not mean other kinds of opposition can be ruled out. For Parker and Slaughter, teamworking is merely the new means by which Taylorism and neo-Human Relations can work more effectively (ibid.).

This approach correctly locates the development of teamwork as a new management strategy that recognises the need to achieve worker commitment in order to increase surplus value through the intensification of labour. However, the difficulty is that it leaves untheorised how workers come to identify with a system which is so exploitative and repressive. There is no investigation of the way that organisational arrangements are designed to achieve this subordination at work. Management-by-stress is clearly distinguishable from the old neo-Human Relations and neo-Taylorist approaches used by Peugeot, Citroën and Simca, as chronicled by Doray (1988). But precisely because it goes so far beyond these in the level of work intensity, the role of employee commitment in the face of this onslaught is all the more remarkable. It is not that Nissan uses neo-Human

Relations approaches because of the need to accommodate the awful level of work intensity, but that these are integrated into the social organisation of work itself— the teams. In addition, it is because teams are used that work can be be so intensive.

It is the insertion of the teamworking social philosophy and practices into organisational and technical practices that allows constant jacking up or lowering of work tempo at management's will. Therefore what we want to understand is not just how management-by-stress ratchets up work at will and individualises workers (which it does), but in addition what is the nature of subjectivity as it relates to managerial strategies—i.e. the role of identity on the line? In this regard there is a contradiction at the heart of Parker and Slaughter's argument between a view which holds that teamwork is an obvious sham, and a view that it appeals to workers' sense of dignity—although this appeal, they argue, is never satisfied.

There can be no doubt that the teamwork devised by auto makers does little to cultivate unambiguous feelings of dignity and mutual respect, or that it functions to increase the rate of exploitation. Nor can it be doubted that it reinforces neo-Taylorist (separation of execution and design) and neo-Human Relations forms of control too (reconstitution of the work group around social and organ- isational imperatives which legitimate this separation). What cannot be con- vincingly maintained is that it functions in the ways it does so as to simply 'con' people that hard work, in the management definition of their daily grind, is good for them.

This is not to deny, incidentally, that management-by-stress inhibits the forma- tion of oppositional class identities, because it certainly does. As we said, Parker and Slaughter's description of the way it works is reasonable enough, especially since they recognise the appeal of teamworking to the development of employees' own identities on the line. But describing the reality of this process—of the manu- facturing of identity between the company and the workforce—as a sophisticated managerial trick unfortunately fails to develop the point they themselves seek to make: individual commitment to work is developed in the search for personal dignity *at* work. Another way of making this point is to say that Parker and Slaughter, while recognising the importance people find in establishing their subjectivity on the line, see this search as illusory because companies use the desire for autonomy and control as a means of entrapping workers in schemes that deliver support in a way which further empowers management. In this sense personal fulfilment, if it exists, is chimeric in quality. Significant research from the US auto industry illustrates that workers do ensnare themselves and feel intense disillusion with the whole process when they realise what is going on. Thus, personal fulfilment does not follow from teamworking schemes, and rarely do workers, the point above accepted, actively seek teamwork strategies:

> Team concept claims to provide workers with dignity, security, and control over their jobs. So why aren't workers aggressively demanding the team concept? In most instances where the team concept has been

implemented, it was a management proposal which met opposition from the workforce.

(ibid., p. 5)

Yet even though this may hold in many cases, it does not explain why workers *do* feel a sense of belonging. In the less typical greenfield scenario, for example at Nissan, worker commitment to the team concept has to be seen in the light of its acceptance by individuals prior to the start of their contract. Therefore employee consent goes hand-in-hand with agreement on the overall package. Clearly, acceptance cannot be explained in terms of management-by-stress alone.

MANAGEMENT-BY-STRESS ALONE?

The really important thing about teamwork is that it is a Human Relations answer to the problems posed by the need to ensure subjective commitment to the kind of very stressful working environment created by JIT. On the one hand, argue Parker and Slaughter, the sheer stress of the workload makes it easier for workers to be picked out and thus picked off, if they create a problem in production. On the other hand it does not matter that workers do *not* agree with the set-up, because the de-skilling routines calculated in the JIT system make everyone easily expendable. But the problem remains, that the ethos of teamwork in certain organisations, in our case at Nissan, highlights the fact that commitment to management-by-stress is generated via teamwork.

Another difficulty which follows from Parker and Slaughter's argument is that workers' real subjectivities and identities could only truly be realised when they act in terms of radical class notions of dignity. Again, we do not deny the arguments they make, that:

1   Teamwork as a management strategy seeks to raise the rate of exploitation.
2   Teamwork seeks to appropriate notions of community and solidarity that make life more tolerable.
3   Teamwork enhances management control.
4   Teamwork takes away much of the dignity people experience at work.
5   The language of teamwork is often less than genuine, and indeed it has to be (see Chapter 3).

However, the question to be answered is why do many other workers, like some of those we interviewed, feel autonomous, independent and emotionally sustained by their experience of teamwork? We do not deny that in pursuing the company's scheme of things, workers' subordination is increased; there are certainly plenty of examples, as our interviewees in Chapter 5 demonstrate, where workers have no commitment, other than a pecuniary one, to Nissan. But the point is, we need to explain how and why people can consent to their own subordination.

It is by accounting for subordination in terms of the identities workers carve out for themselves that commitment to work can be explained. More than this, we can begin to see exactly how insecure the system itself is in delivering the substance of people's desires without explaining insecurity (solely) in terms of union betrayal. Even if the latter were true, it cannot explain why teamwork successfully appeals to some people's wants, even when countervailing forces are present. This does not deny our point, made often, that it is the absence of alternative world views that allows company notions to prevail. Where individual workers feel isolated and see the world other than through company eyes, there is no counter-culture in which these alternative views can develop. Joe, from 'final trim and chassis', described what was a common sense of frustration with the union's lack of visibility. For him and others we interviewed, being a union member was an important point of principle even though it might not mean much in practice. His response tells us a great deal about why individuals might not find union membership appealing, even though they might not always agree with the company:

Q: Are you in the union?

Joe: I am a member of the AEU—for what it's worth, like.

Q: Are you just an ordinary member?

Joe: Just an ordinary member, but as I say it's [membership subscription] deducted from the wage but that is the only thing I ever see—there is no contact from the union. In fact you just go to work and you never see anything else—you just go to your particular department, come out at night and that is it.

Q: Is anybody else in your particular group in the AEU?

Joe: Yeah, there is at least one out of five of us, perhaps another two. They feel pretty much like me you know—they are pretty much ambivalent, thinking that the union is pretty much toothless—it's got no strength.

Q: If it did have a more active role would that make a difference to people?

Joe: Oh yeah! There is one bloké in particular who is pretty strong on the union too [as well as me]. He is in the union . . . he steps back a bit from saying too much but unionwise he likes to cause bother in other ways by opening his mouth, but it never goes further than words, like—how can it?

Q: What about the Company Council?

Joe: The Company Council! That is a complete shambles that thing—it always just gives you the company line. You just get what the company wants—the odd bit of change here and there maybe.

That this state of affairs can persist says much about the union's lack of an alternative vision—indeed, lack of independence. At the same time, however, it is important to recognise that while unions lead workers into the team set-up— Parker and Slaughter's aim is to reject the incorporativist strategies of the union hierarchy (the UAW)—and while the things they lead them into are real enough to assist in the empowerment of management, some workers are often agreeing to things which they see as bestowing dignity on them. For example Jim, a welder, was pleased that working for Nissan gave him a sense of worth and a status he felt was missing when he worked as a boilermaker at NESL (North East Shipbuilders Limited).

Nevertheless, only a minority of those whom we spoke to perceive the 'Nissan Way' as bestowing any special kind of dignity on them. Yet Nissan ways of working are seen as legitimate by most *where they continue the institutions which create consensus (kaizen,* teamwork, etc.), for they offer things that are attractive such as the perception of involvement. These institutions which bestow respect and dignity are double-edged, for they have to deliver very scarce resources (really in the form of promotion and job security) to continue to succeed. Finally, it should be remembered that those workers who found the company attractive were those who had felt 'looked after' so far. Jimmy, for example, felt vindicated when he made what at the time appeared a 'daft' decision to his mates, exchanging what they saw as the 'cushy' ways of the Navy for what looked like a hard and stressful job at Nissan:

Jimmy: The good thing about Nissan is the family thing. . . . Not just the company family, like, but the whole thing. They do everything for the family too—last Christmas they hired the Metrocentre for the kids.

People like Jimmy had had little or no confrontation with management. Those who had, very quickly recognised teamwork in terms Parker and Slaughter would find familiar. This is hardly surprising because Wickens makes it clear that Nissan is only concerned with those who view the company in *its* terms.

The truth is that this need to be at one with the company is too common an aspect of life at Nissan to be seen as anything other than systemic in origin. That is to say, there is often disillusion, and this derives from failure in the internal competition between workers and hence a loss of morale and status. This competition then is contradictory—many succeed but others fail. But then this only serves to reveal a deeper truth about teamwork, quality and flexibility—that they serve for the creation of a consensus for all, where all agree. If not, one's own interpretation of needs and search for dignity are irrelevant, for they are not company defined. Far from promoting harmony and dignity for all, Nissan's teamwork promotes personal insecurity and anxiety for some.

TEAMWORK, CONSENT AND SELF-SUBORDINATION

If we can describe flexibility and quality as the organisational and technical means by which the company seeks to ensure subordination, control, surveillance and exploitation, teamwork represents the critical social form in which workers consent to these processes of domination. Teamwork depends precisely upon self-subordination for it shifts the locus of control onto individuals, who perceive themselves as guardians of quality and flexibility. This is a powerful operationalisation of control for it depoliticises domination where it is seen as linked solely to line speed—not to the manager or the company. Another powerful device for maintaining control by means of individualised (and therefore depoliticised) surveillance is the so-called Neighbour Check code. This works by identifying fellow workers who are perceived as miscreants, responsible for poor quality on the line. It can only work because a strong corporate identity is present, and this is precisely where teamworking comes in. For Nissan, an effective team is one which can instil the ingredients of what the company perceives as collective working practices:

Features of an effective team

- A good team has a high success rate
- A good team agrees clear, challenging objectives
- A good team has a leader
- A good team has a mix of skill and knowledge. A group of people who co-operate together on a task can accomplish more than the sum total of the individuals
- A good team creates a supportive atmosphere. . . . Where people are happy to go at risk. . . . Can say what they think. . . . Develop upon each other's ideas. . . . Be committed to an agreed course of action— even though there may be differences of opinions
- A good team learns from experiences . . . [of] both success and failure
- A good team works hard and plays hard

(source: 'Features of an effective team', *Kaizen Leader Training Manual*)

Teamworking is the social form in which quality and flexibility are used to subordinate workers. At the same time, the practical and ideological working of teams legitimises the company's deployment of quality and flexibility to this end. Before looking at how this is effected, it will be useful if we turn to what Nissan have to say about teamworking and how it is interpreted by the Director of Personnel.

The role of teamworking and its purpose, according to Nissan, is to:

recognise that all staff have a valued contribution to make as individuals but in addition [we] believe that this contribution can be most effective

within a teamworking environment. . . . Our aim is to build a company
with which people can identify and to which they feel commitment.

(cited in Wickens, 1987, p. 76)

The most interesting things here are the following: what does 'valued contribution' of individuals mean and how is it used in practice to elicit consent? Following
our assertion above, why and how is teamworking of primary significance to this
process of consensus building and how exactly does it link into the nature of individual identity and commitment at work? In fact, individuality is important to
Nissan only is so far as 'all employees [should be] committed to the aims of the
Company, i.e., recognising that each individual has a valued contribution to
make' (ibid.). This contribution, however, is valued only where 'everyone [is]
working in the same direction' (ibid.). Mutual trust and mutual respect are sentiments that Nissan holds dear.

Wickens (1987, ch. 6) argues that teams allow for both employee dignity and
mutual respect between managers and subordinates in a way that helps the company and the employee together. His examples of NUMMI and Volvo are drawn
to illuminate his thesis that in spite of profound differences between the respective
histories and philosophies of the US and Swedish manufacturers, the team concept makes both GM-Toyota and Volvo successful. We shall consider the actual
working of teams at Nissan later in this chapter, but fundamentally we are concerned with why and how teams work. Wickens demonstrates great company
modesty when, in the context of *why* it works, he claims to be somewhat bewil-
dered by the success of the team concept in general: 'Teamworking and commitment are difficult to define but you know it when you see it, or perhaps more
accurately, *feel it*' (ibid., p. 95; emphasis added).

This is an invitation to enlightenment which we are keen to respond to. But
perhaps he does understand the essence of teamworking more than he is prepared
to allow for. He belies his awe at the workings of the process, its origins and
purpose, when he continues: 'Teamworking is not dependent on people working
in groups but upon everyone working toward the same aims and objectives' (ibid.,
p. 95). In a sentence, this view sums up both the objective of the organisation—an
imposition of a particular definition of teamwork—and the impetus, or rationale,
for the social character of teamwork in the company. This places great pressure on
individuals to pull together for the common good. However, people find that
teamworking at Nissan actually leads to a lot of individual competitiveness. In the
words of Gary, 'You have to look good and be good'. Gary feels that this pressure
to always do things on the company's terms creates a good deal of competitive
tension and personal anguish within the team:

Gary: You have always got to impress people. I mean you might have all the best
ideas in the world, but if someone hears of them and goes and tells the gaffer then
he sounds like the good bloke. There is a lot of pressure and that type of thing.

And this kind of pressure to be at once open for the company yet competitive with workmates causes much individual anxiety and insecurity. It is difficult always to trust people who may themselves be just as anxious to avoid failure as oneself.

HOW DOES IT LOOK IN PRACTICE?

Approximately 3000 manufacturing staff and technicians work on the assembly line (or track), demarcated in working areas, or zones. Each zone contains a number of teams of between ten and twenty workers. Within each team, workers are assigned a broad range of operational duties including maintenance and sub-assembly tasks. Nissan defines these operations as multi-skilled and therefore considers its workers as functionally flexible. The experience of line workers suggests that this flexibility is of a limited kind, as the quotation from Terry in Chapter 3 indicates (see p. 83).

Workers are invariably tied to specific teams whose range of 'skills' is limited, except in the sense described previously. That is, workers who remain in the same team for any period of time find that they have appropriated a number of 'skills' ranging from the general development of their physical dexterity to know-how necessary to do the job not only adequately, but better than that defined by the 'Standard Operation' pro forma (ESO, op. cit.). Indeed, Nissan, as we pointed out previously, recognises that the integrity of teams requires commitment from specific individuals. At most, movement of labour is about the incorporation of new members into teams as new initiates into the company, and of limited horizontal movement between teams carrying out a similar range of cognate duties, for example welding operations or sub-assembly routines. It is precisely because the functioning of teams demands a fair degree of *inflexibility* in terms of the movement of personnel and up-skilling that so much attention is paid to teamwork ideology. If anything, workers' experience of teamwork, coupled with the role of quality and workers' self-supervision of quality, is of quite a rigid system of social organisation and control. Parker and Slaughter's argument about reconciling individual specialisms in a team is worth recalling at this juncture in view of what Nissan has to say about the team:

> Organisations are about people working together to achieve a common objective. In our case it's about 'build the best quality car in Europe'. Therefore we need to develop teams, a team can accomplish much more than the sum of its individual members. Teamwork is individuals working together to accomplish more than they could alone, but more than that it can be exciting, satisfying and enjoyable. If any of us were given the task of building the England football team—we know the task would involve much more than just picking the best eleven players in England.

The success of the team would depend not only on individual skill but the way those individuals supported and worked with each other.

(Nissan, *Kaizen Leader Training Manual*)

The last sentence, together with the view that 'individuals working together . . . accomplish more than they could alone', represents what Nissan and management consultants describe as 'synergy'. Synergy is a resource for all organisations because it represents the appropriation, to the company's benefit, of what commonly happens in work organisations where workers help one another, perhaps to fulfil quotas, or to allow someone to 'have a break'. With the team concept in operation, the use of 'synergy' is a recognition of the importance the company attaches to the harnessing of what this 'helping out' depends upon—the social and psychological factors that help create group or worker solidarity. It is this which Nissan, via the team concept, utilises for the company's own ends. It relies upon a carefully articulated set of definitions about both teams and teamworking, and the relationship of individuals to teams: both the individual and his or her work only have a meaning in so far as it is specified by the company.

THE SOCIAL IMPORTANCE OF THE TEAM: WHAT'S IN A WORD?

An obvious social and psychological implication is that one's relationship to others in the team has to be defined by the company's imperatives. This is an important political and strategic point. It is political because it is a recognition that since in reality flexibility is quite limited, workers in teams are bound to build up close relationships at work. It is strategic for two reasons:

1. As a consequence of the formation of personal and social identities in the team, the company needs to control or moderate their potentially disruptive character (sometimes, as our interviewees point out, disruption does occur—in spite of the teamwork ideology).
2. The JIT system, because of its abandonment of buffer stocks in its tight technological cycles, is extremely susceptible to social disruption. The latter can occur, either through organised or unorganised activity. However, because of the role of personal identification/responsibility for quality, including the surveillance effect of the Neighbour Check code, it is very difficult for individuals to commit sabotage. This being the case, how does the company attempt to ensure that its view of reality prevails?

The first, most obvious method for ensuring tight control is in the preliminary stages of recruitment, when 'undesirables', or people whose faces are deemed not to fit, can be excluded. However, as we discovered to our surprise, it did not stop some 'committed' trade unionists from getting in. Morgan and Sayer (1988) provide an interesting analysis of the impact of new management practices and New Realism on labour activism in South Wales. Another way is carefully to define everyone's social and psychological roles. By recognising the relative inflexibility that teamworking generates, Nissan is tacitly accepting a degree of potential organisational instability. How is the management strategy for control advanced and what does it consist of?

By judiciously imposing its description of the social and psychological characteristics of what makes for good team members, in a language which we all feel comforted by, Nissan explicitly identifies dependence upon the harmonious internal character of team dynamics. It is a signal of how much store Nissan puts by the social role of teamwork. In addition, it is a recognition of the importance workers attach to determinate relations of support and dependence from one another at work.

That it does not work out quite like this is attributable to the inability of Nissan, or any work organisation, to circumvent the uncomfortable reality that is the tedium of assembly-line routines. By an act of ideological wordplay, vital not just at Nissan but with team concept companies everywhere, workers are told what they always knew, in terms that devalue the very collective significance of workers' experiences. This process takes individuals' commonsense notions of teamworking and the actions involved, then twists them to the company's benefit. What makes for an effective team? We are told that one of the vital ingredients is added when the lucky person who displays leadership characteristics can achieve a dominant position in the team. Secondly, it requires others, with equally important but distinctive psychological and social characteristics, to find their appropriate place in the team hierarchy. As the *Kaizen Leader Training Manual* says: 'It is a combination of different roles within the team that seems a crucial factor in its success.' These other roles are defined by the homely titles of 'doer', 'thinker' and 'carer'.

Doers, thinkers and carers in teamworking

'Doer'
- Doers are action centred people.
- They constantly urge people to get on with the task in hand.
- They tend to be totally concerned with the task ('the what') often at the expense of the process ('the how').
- They are often impatient with 'waffle' and tend to swing into action without thinking things through.

'Thinker'

- Thinkers are good at producing carefully considered ideas.
- Weighing up alternative courses of action based upon other people's ideas.
- Rarely have much to say—they are often amongst the quietest members of the team.
- When they do speak they are the sort of people who come up with winning ideas.
- If they are listened to.

'Carer'

- Carers are people oriented.
- They tend to be alert to relationship issues within the team.
- Good at easing tension and maintaining harmony.
- Carers help the leader to counterbalance the doers and thinkers who both tend to be task—not people—oriented.

(source: *Kaizen Leader Training Manual*)

It seems, however, that these paternalistic and maternalistic characteristics are insufficient to allow democratic decision-making to prevail. Individuals can be trusted when the 'carers' and 'thinkers' stick to their place in the scheme of things. However, the really important people are the 'doers'. These individuals are people who, once wound-up, can be guaranteed to get the job done. Better if, in the end, we all get on and do the job. Just to emphasise Nissan's revelation: we cannot agree to disagree, for, in the end, what matters is that we follow the leader(s). Leaders can adapt their mode of leadership from 'participative' to 'autocratic' depending upon the situation they are dealing with (see below). And this is the rub. It sounds benevolent to let people feel emotionally cared for when their own psychological dispositions are seemingly taken into account. Terms like 'doers', 'carers', 'thinkers' and 'leaders' represent what makes healthy families tick and great countries better! However, most workers assume this means they will be treated as adults, with power and discretion, in addition to responsibility; in other words, that they can be allowed to disagree on the fundamental issues in their working lives. But that only happens in democracies and in democratically run work organisations. The latter would allow people to act as individuals *and* to disagree, or rather, to put it in the present context, agree to disagree. However, Nissan's consensus has little to do with democracy or dissent at any level: '6–10 people each with different views who fail to cohere or who simply proceed by letting the majority prevail (as in voting) are a group, (i.e. collection of individuals) not a team' (Nissan, *What Is a Team?*, p. 2). If the company says it's true it must be.

This is a vital issue in the teamwork concept as operated by Nissan, for it gets right to the heart of the matter. The people who implement decision-making are the leaders (team leaders in the first instance, then supervisors). Where the team cannot reach a decision—which would appear a reasonably common and under- standable circumstance—a consensus must be imposed (which is hardly a con- sensus). Nissan suggests that this is possible where time is pressing—but when, on a busy line, would it not be?

The reality behind the rhetoric is different. If it were true that line workers could openly discuss issues of working methods and procedures, important or unimportant, it would naturally lead to disagreement, the probability of a final consensus notwithstanding. The very idea of a consensus is that it allows for those who agree to disagree to get on with their differences, while fully participating in the efficient prosecution of high-quality organisational objectives (as we shall demonstrate). This is a perfectly possible and desirable outcome of real—as opposed to manufactured—participation in organisations. But this type of partici- pation would assume employee control and determination of organisational strategies. At Nissan, if it were true that employees really do take part in the decision-making process, in other words that they are treated as citizens, not corporate souls, with the rights and not just the responsibilities which the com- pany is always keen to spell out, their discussions would couple real deliberation and actual participation with employee-centred control. Accordingly, there would be no problem with the role of dissent in the context of specific methods and procedures. For we must remember that it is not just that individuals must accept the company philosophy lock, stock and barrel, but even the very form of their disagreements must be articulated on company terms. If this was not so, why would such great store be set by the careful description of the role of 'the leader'? In fact, it is the account of the role of the 'leader', more than any other role, which belies, contrary to the rhetoric, claims about everyone being treated with respect as individuals. The priority of company-determined imperatives comes through:

> In difficult situations, where a consensus cannot be reached or where time is important [the leader is someone who is] leading from the front by deciding what needs to be done.
> An effective leader is concerned both with the task (the 'what') and with the decision making process (the 'how'). A leader also uses a range of different styles from participative through to consultative. Even tending to be autocratic depending upon the situation.

> (ibid., p. 3)

EMPOWERMENT AND TEAMWORKING: THE LEGITIMATION OF AUTOCRATIC LEADERSHIP

An autocratic style is what most line workers experience. Indeed, given the lack of real discussion about the work process—usually no more than ten minutes per day—and the reality of an organisational and market strategy determined from above, it is little wonder that the 'autocratic' leadership style prevails over the 'participative' and the 'consultative'. In the *Kaizen Activity Work and Answer Sheets*, we can see how this classic attempt to legitimise undemocratic strategies by coding them in terms of their opposite is rationalised and legitimised. We can consider just one of these, the 'lost at sea' scenario. It is a fun game which members can play in one of their *kaizen* meetings. It functions as an exercise in teamwork decision-making, where 'life-saving' priorities are asserted by individuals and group decisions are adhered to by all. The game begins by asking team members to pretend they are lost in a boat at sea. They have a number of items in their possession, such as a mirror, a sextant, a quart of rum, a flare gun and a bottle for collecting water. These items in the game have properties, the full extent of which we have only limited knowledge. It is not immediately obvious that a mirror is of more use than a sextant unless: (a) we have been in the situation before—or played the game before; (b) we are fully aware of the relative properties of the variables in relation to one another; (c) we can fully appreciate how the interaction of the team members might make better use of one, as opposed to another, of the variables; and (d) we can interlink (b) and (c). After the group has made its decision about which of these items would best help its members survive, the team leader goes through each of the items, assessing the relative merits of each. By a process of elimination, based on the leader's knowledge about the benefits of each item, the group is then told the right answer, which may or may not concur with their own.

In practice, this is really an exercise designed to promote or legitimise this form of decision-making—consultation, which is really an autocratic process of informing and imposing the pre-ordained 'right' answer. Whether the team's answer was the same as the leader's is beside the point. The vital issue is that they have all discussed the rights and wrongs of the different items on the basis of limited knowledge. Discussing things among members of the group is a good thing, certainly, but it hardly makes for democracy if real decision-making lies elsewhere. What this game-playing represents is an attempt to educate employees in a particular view of what democracy and participation at work entails. It is clear that this is a fairly limited form of both democracy and participation. But it acquires legitimacy because it involves individuals in the process of agreeing to carry out already determined decisions. This is an important process of legitimation which seeks to define participation and democracy within closely circumscribed terms: the 'games' are about learning to participate in the agreement of pre-ordained decisions, rather than education for really democratic participation which would involve deliberation and choice about what the range of options for action might be. The important thing is that all the team members have been involved in agreeing collectively on the 'right' answer, which is confirmed or rejected by the team leader. Yet the group can only act on information at its disposal, and the team leader is the source of that knowledge. This, of course, mirrors the organisation itself, which in that sense could be said to work on a 'need to know' basis down the hierarchy and along the line.

Exercises and game-playing are an ideological ploy used in all companies utilising the teamwork concept. The real agenda is that actual decision-making occurs elsewhere (where time allows!) exactly as in the 'lost at sea' game. It's good fun, we all play. But there is only one answer, known in advance. Of course, if you have played before, you know the answer, or rather, the methods. If everyone knew that 'one quart of rum' came last, we would hardly need to vote to decide, and since majority decisions (democracy) are not what the team concept implies by participation, clearly the aim is to teach us *not* what we already know, but to get us collectively to absorb the right answer—how to do the job, how fast we should do it, where we should do it—in short, the How, When and Where over which line workers have no power.

In a manufacturing environment where workers had sufficient control and determination of their environment, the answer would not come down from above, but would be arrived at on the basis of the common knowledge of the team members after due consideration of one another's skills. There might even be different, equally appropriate 'right' answers. Some of our respondents emphasised that in many instances, even though they could provide better ways to perform tasks, these were frequently ignored, or deferred until *kaizen* meetings, where the idea met with greater or lesser degrees of success. Even though someone could perform a task better, if that person was unable to generalise his or her knowledge by properly explaining its actions and effects, it would be rejected. This is also a common finding among researchers of the US automotive industry, where similar teamworking strategies are rather more advanced than in the UK and Europe (Parker and Slaughter, 1988; Lichtenstein and Meyer, 1989).

The purpose of game-playing exercises, as it is defined by Nissan in the *Kaizen Activity Work and Answer Sheets*, is to provide a model for team members of what decision-making, Nissan style, amounts to. Together with other game sets, it provides powerful images which disclose the rules of conduct in the company's decision-making process. It fulfils this aim by carefully telling participants what to do and how to behave. It is in many ways similar to schoolroom games designed to educate people in the whys and wherefores of parliamentary democracy. There is a specific appraisal of what can and cannot be expected from group members. If this kind of activity serves as one of the ideological modes by which autocratic leadership and social subordination are legitimised, then the equally carefully defined roles of 'carer', 'thinker' and 'doer' serve as the lifesize expression of 'responsible' participation and involvement. These three figures of respectability serve, in effect, to naturalise individual subordination to the paternalistic leader figure. 'Carers', 'thinkers' and 'doers' know their place in the world and in the world of work. It is up to individuals themselves to identify with these roles, otherwise the company will do it for them. The exercise, in defining what is and is not acceptable involvement in the decision-making process, depends on a limitation of the scope of real involvement. This serves to tell workers how to reach a consensus.

To paraphrase the *Kaizen Leader Training Manual*, Nissan's view about this, we have drawn out the four main features of what Nissan considers responsible participation to consist of:

1   Do not push your own views on colleagues.
2   Do not just support something because it is easier to go along with the majority.
3   Do not avoid conflict if it is inherent in the situation and do not compromise for fear of prolonging the issue.
4   Different opinions help rather than hinder.

These four 'guidelines' for the most part appear laudable. However, what can a 'doer' make of 1–4? Will he or she be able to respond as well as the 'carer' or the 'thinker'? Most employees simply what to be good 'doers' because real participation is lacking. (How often are you going to be able to design the social organisation and physical character of the factory where you are employed?)

KAIZEN AS TEAM BUILDING FOR CONSENSUS AND SELF-SUBORDINATION

> The kaizen philosophy assumes the total involvement of all employees, but recognises that the success of active participation depends upon individuals feeling that they are part of the 'Nissan way'.
>
> (Nissan, *Kaizen Leader Training Manual*, 'Introduction')

It is in *kaizen* that employees learn the 'Nissan Way' in its full ideological glory. *Kaizen* takes workers out of the line to give them what Nissan calls skill, quality experience and development. It is in the *kaizen* teams that individuals learn that personal contributions to the development of the labour process must be carefully tailored and articulated in a company-sanctioned discourse. This realisation directs workers' thoughts and attitudes towards a corporate response when the desired level of output is required by the company. At the same time, this strategy is designed to individualise and effectively isolate people as individuals within the 'family' of Nissan. Here, one is taught to respond as a company-defined individual. One is first and foremost a Nissan worker, one of that precious band, 'that unique group of people that makes up Nissan Motor Manufacturing (UK) Ltd.' (ibid.).

The 'doers', 'carers' and 'thinkers', who learn their place in the scheme of things, who have set about improving quality and (as a perceived bonus) developing their skills, can be put back on to the assembly-line to continue to work in the 'Nissan Way'. It would be truly difficult to over-emphasise this finding. On more than one occasion, workers told us of situations, both during *kaizen* groups and morning team meetings, where their presentation of views and criticisms was only acceptable if 'done according to the book' (Jonathan). It is hardly unusual for corporations to speak of their concern for individual integrity and dignity while pursuing the opposite course in practice. As in other such cases company claims about the promotion of individuality need to be treated with a healthy degree of scepticism.

The objective, then, is for *kaizen* to teach company lore about quality. Learning about quality is explained as helping both the company and the worker. Through the process of teamwork, the latter is supposed to experience enhanced skill. But as we said above, what is really happening is that the commitment to the team process leads to managerial acquisition of worker knowledge with no cost to the company. In other words, it is a way of syphoning off task know-how. Workers are made to feel good and rewarded with the promise of security, status and power (skill), for this is what they are told *kaizen* activity promotes in addition to quality. Workers back on the line, having gone through *kaizen*, keep a check on one another through the Neighbour Check system, which can be seen as a form of self-policing, illustrated below. With the philosophy of individual responsibility for quality and the ideology of subordination to the corporate ethos instilled at *kaizen* meetings, morning team talks and supervision/team leader monitoring, peer group surveillance fits neatly and easily into the needs of the tripod (quality, flexibility and teamwork).

'Quality' is drummed into people at *kaizen* meetings, which, as we have argued, are organised to appropriate workers' ideas and legitimate employer determination of line speed and organisation. The general commitment to teamworking, as analysed above, represents the social and organisational fulcrum of this new social control as mediated in the company's discourse on quality. Thus perceived, team-work enmeshes workers in the social organisation of the company view of the world, where they accept the terms and conditions of the contract—security and prospects together with respect and dignity in exchange for personal commitment to the Nissan ethos: quality, flexibility, teamwork. By the time workers get to work on the line, the battle for hearts and minds has been won. The point, however, is to keep on winning, and the paraphernalia of teamworking tries to sustain this.

So far we have looked critically at the claims made by Nissan about the role played by teams in creating a humane workplace and a highly marketable product. In addition, we have argued that to understand how they operate requires an understanding of the special social and psychological importance attributed to the ideas of quality, flexibility and teamwork. These ideas involve very powerful assumptions about the purpose of work; they do so by initiating a particular set of social and psychological relations between individual workers. We shall now consider what these are and how they link together.

TOTAL QUALITY MANAGEMENT FOR TOTAL MANAGEMENT CONTROL

What the social and psychological relations referred to above help to contrive are institutions of togetherness and cooperativeness on the company's terms. These institutions include *kaizen* meetings, morning team briefings and other sets of institutions such as those referred to earlier: company-sponsored sports and social events, for example. It is not enough to get to team meetings to agree to give knowledge of the job away for free, nor to give up precious unpaid time before and after work to clean up before the next shift. Another side of the process of subordination needs to be worked through before managerial control can be properly consummated.

The catalyst in the operation of the quality–flexibility–teamwork tripod is more than workers being keen, happy and fulfilled. Assembly-line work is pretty dull for most people most of the time, quite apart from its heavy, dirty and dangerous qualities. To make the system of control, surveillance and exploitation function properly, one needs a set of institutions organised specifically so that workers themselves can participate in them. Workers are only really considered full team members when they prove they can run the quality system themselves. Following our argument above, where quality is concerned with social control, in those cases where workers, as part of the requirement of the operation of quality in work (Total Quality Control), are proactive in establishing this day-in, day-out, they are mediating the terms of their own subordination. There is no room for negotiating these terms. They are clearly laid down in a system of tight peer group assessment.

The strength of this system is that it is legitimated by the seeming reasonableness of every other part of the tripod—quality, efficiency, responsibility for the customer; dignity for all through respect for one another's work and performance. *Kaizen* teaches company loyalty and paternalism, the line team teaches individual control and the company view of group solidarity, while 'quality' is the great ideological shibboleth in pursuit of which individual workers collaborate in the process of their own subordination. This process, prefigured in *kaizen* and team working *per se*, is guaranteed by four institutions which coexist with, and in some respects define, different moments in the social organisation of the labour process. These are:

1 'Help lamps'
2 'Neighbour Check'
3 'Visible Management System'—quality, volume, cost
4 'Quality Targets'

For workers to control quality, control needs a name. The name Nissan uses to express a benign view of the operation of quality is 'Total Quality Control'. (See, for example, Oakland, 1989, for an example of current thinking on the nature of quality in the production process from the new management perspective.) 'Total Quality Control' is intended to ensure that 'the theme of quality runs through every aspect of the business'. More interestingly, for our argument about the contours of self-subordination, Nissan says: 'Quality is not something that is left to quality controllers, but is the responsibility of every single person at the plant and everyone has a significant contribution to make' (Nissan Information Pack, 1988).

The four aspects of this process of Total Quality Control together form a package of instructions, attitudes and institutions which provide for, and consummate, self-subordination as a necessary corollary to the overall process of subordination. Teamworking, in *kaizen* and on the line, as defined in company ideology for the promotion of quality, is a process in which workers control one another's actions. It is this which gives to the autocratic internal regime a spurious air of employee participation and control in work. However, it is not the kind of control which leads to employee empowerment at work, but rather to forms of self-control and peer control that inhibit individual development and control of work. The four elements of control are as follows.

'Help lamps'

> A wire running the whole length of the production line can be pulled at any time by an operator who has a 'Quality Concern'. This activates a siren and a flashing light and draws the attention of a supervisor who can investigate the area of concern and take the appropriate action.
>
> (ibid., p. 8)

The claim here is that workers will halt the line to ensure that 'poor quality' items are dealt with before another team (or set of 'customers') downstream receives the unit. But another interpretation could also be placed upon the 'help lamps' and is supported by many of those whom we interviewed. To begin with, all noted the enormous stress which the lamps placed them under. The stress they described derived from a fear that continual interruptions further down the line would identify them as incompetent. In addition, workers would often rectify faults created by others upstream because frequent operation of the help lamp for minor defects might itself be mistaken for incompetence and the resultant check of all work could also reveal defects of their own making. As our interviewee Joan put it:

Joan: Work must be perfect; we check each other's work as it is passed down the line. A single fault getting by leads to the whole lot having to be checked. If faults get through, they are traced back to the line and even the [individual] worker.

It is clear that many of these faults are niggling and would not even be noticed by the customer, let alone matter to the product. Though management might like to argue that these 'corrections' arise out of pride in the product and have nothing to do with stress or fear of chastisement, this cosy one-dimensional view simply is not shared by all employees. Pride there may be, but this has to be measured against the high fear-of-failure factor. As well as pride and fear, workers also express a weariness at having to rectify others' errors. In this instance, they have access to the homely institution of Neighbour Check.

Neighbour Check

This is the second element of the social control system and it is at the heart of the self-subordination system:

> The philosophy running through the production process . . . is that no defect will pass from one part of the process to the next. In a series of 'Neighbour Checks', whenever one component or sub-assembly is to be passed onto the next station or 'neighbour' it is checked by the operator. By building up this network the integrity of the manufactured quality is continuously developed within the process.

(ibid., p. 9)

Not only do workers pick up on others' faults, Neighbour Check encourages a competitive relationship between individuals and teams. This stressful situation is inherent in Nissan's operation of teamworking practices. Workers feel they have to pick up on others' faults because the same sniping happens to them. A kind of competition between teams sometimes develops. This is the case despite the powerful ideological apparatuses which weigh down on employees, from initiation onwards. In fact, this competition is, like everything else that the company extols and the employees resent, interpreted as a search for 'quality'. However, knowing what we do about the role of quality in the process of social control, it is clear that the Neighbour Check code is a means for legitimising peer group surveillance of individual activity in the production process.

To keep this pressure up and to legitimise it as part of the drive for quality, as part of the search for a product which most customers can enjoy, faults are coded in the form of an index. So that this sniping between employees plays its intended part, it needs to be linked to an objective measurement system of personal and group performance that allows it to be seen as a device for ensuring quality rather than control. The way this works is very interesting. The team leader will not tell you that the left-hand door is slightly misaligned. Rather, 'faults' are marked by the downstream team and at the end of the line, each vehicle is accorded a score. The score for the car is the basis of the score given to each operative on the line. For example, problems with paintwork or welding will be traced back to the place (and hence the individual) from which they originated. This system is known as the Vehicle Evaluation System.

The Neighbour Check code, then, fulfils two functions in the syndrome of quality as a mechanism of social control. First, it represents the most visible social form in which the team acts to regulate individual behaviour. It can do this because the autocratic and paternalistic lessons about correct behaviour learnt at *kaizen* and in the general company philosophy find their concrete expression in those relations (described above) which are fostered to promote quality—being a good worker in the 'Nissan Way' as a 'doer', 'carer' and so on. Thus, Neighbour Check provides an everyday reminder of the benefits of being a good worker. It is the weapon *par excellence* which helps the company maintain its control.

The second function of Neighbour Check is that it represents the success of Nissan's control strategy. It serves to consummate this control where workers themselves are the actors at the centre of the subordination process. Again, the legitimation principle demands that all means must serve the end of quality. It is by describing and accounting for this process of subordination as the pursuit of an 'objective' characteristic (quality) that one's continued employment can seem reasonable. This echoes Burawoy's (1979) argument in the sense that subordination by consent is secured through employee adherence to management imperatives. In Burawoy's study, an indulgency pattern—involving employee 'game playing'—was essential if management was to prevail. In the case of Nissan, however, consent is more tightly secured since everyone agrees that quality on management's terms is a good thing. The need to tolerate 'game playing' at Nissan is unnecessary since the game, in this case of the pursuit of quality, is an inherent part of the labour process itself.

The third and fourth components of the Total Quality Control philosophy are identified by two further team and individual evaluation procedures which depend upon competition within and between teams.

Visible management system

The third element of the control system is described as a 'visible management system', which forms that part of the evaluation process for each team which we have just considered: 'On these "Q.V.C." [Quality Volume Cost] quality data and performance are displayed. The graphs and charts are completed by the individual sections and thus the awareness of the need for quality is continuously enhanced' (ibid.).

Quality targets

The fourth feature of Total Quality Control is described as promoting quality via 'quality targets'. While these serve to provide an indicator of overall team performance in chasing targets, their other aim is to promote individual competition and highlight individual shortcomings.

The fourth feature [of this control system] consists of quality targets which are divided into Supervisor sections so that each team of people in the production process has a defined target to aim at and monitor. The targets, which are constantly changed to aim at a constantly improving product, are important in that they make everyone aware of their own individual contribution to the overall philosophy

(ibid.)

At this point, it is worth underlining the main feature of the ideology of the 'Nissan Way'. In our view there is a disjuncture between the appearance and the reality of the organisation's claims about the operation and purpose of its internal work organisation. We can represent this figuratively in relation to claims about the nature of the quality–flexibility–teamwork tripod (Table 2). The tripod, with its emphasis on consensus, raises a number of questions in the light of our findings about some other claims the company makes, in relation to what the public relations department describes as 'Facts against Fallacies' (*Nissan Information Pack*, 1988). We would argue that the realities in Table 2 lie behind appearances as described by Nissan.

Teamwork is thus important in delivering employee control, and in Table 2 we represent Nissan's tripod (plus the role of consensus) as the organisational *sine qua non* of control, surveillance and exploitation. In other ways too, Nissan can be somewhat fanciful in the way it depicts particular features of the organisation which have been challenged by critics. Below, we list some of the instances which we feel shed light on this. In response to Nissan's 'Facts against Fallacies', we present what we feel to be a rather more accurate assessment of some of the real facts, as against Nissan's interpretation of life in their organisation. In place of Nissan's 'Facts against Fallacies', we feel that our 'Realities against Fantasies' better describes the reality of life in the company, as it has been conveyed to us by our interviewees.

Table 2 The contrasting appearance and reality of the main features of the 'Nissan Way'

Appearance (i.e. as Nissan sees its 'tripod', tied together by a fourth element, consensus)	Reality (i.e. behind the appearance)
1. Flexibility	1. In practice, only in terms of cognate tasks within same team
2. Consensus	2. No mechanism for challenging one-dimensional company views. In this sense, consensus must be seen as imposed
3. Quality	3. Used to impose consensus via tight Neighbour Check, QVC and VES (Vehicle Evaluation Score)
4. Teamwork	4. As in 3, also cuts across the potential for solidarity both via individual peer assessment and technical structure (JIT) of hierarchy

Realities against Fantasies

1. 'All overtime is paid' (*Nissan Information Pack*, 1988, p. 2).

In reality, it depends what is meant by overtime. Not all work is considered to be overtime, for instance normal 'housekeeping' which involves preparation and finishing. Cleaning up after work is done in the worker's own time, as is arriving early to set work up.

2. 'The Nissan plant at Sunderland does not operate under Japanese style management' (ibid., p. 3).

Again, it depends what is meant by 'Japanese style' management. Just-In-Time and kanban systems do operate. The union is secondary to the Company Council; and the line of hierarchy and leadership begins with the team leader and continues with the supervisor. Clearly, a new set of management strategies constituted around what are commonly known as Japanese production concepts prevail.

3. 'Flexibility does not mean switching from job to job' (ibid.) (i.e. functional flexibility is limited).

The ability to complete a variety of jobs is a feature of work within departments. For example, within such departments as the paint shop or final trim and chassis, every task has to covered by the team so the team can cope with occasional labour shortage. But this does not presume any degree of up-skilling, whatever Wickens's assertions to the contrary.

THE IDEOLOGY OF THE TRIPOD—THE VIRTUELESS CIRCLE

It is clear, then, that Nissan can often be parsimonious in accounting for the nature of its management style and practice. To the same extent, it can be argued that Wickens's explanation for the organisational virtuosity inherent in the tripod falls short of an entirely satisfactory account of the reasons for its existence and success.

We reached this conclusion after lengthy discussion with our interviewees in the context of our comparative research into the causes and consequences of similar management practices in the USA. In particular, the plant at Sunderland bears close comparison with its Nissan cousin at Smyrna, Tennessee, and the joint venture between General Motors and Toyota at Fremont in California (NUMMI —New United Motors Manufacturing Inc.). The latter especially raises very interesting questions about the role of autonomous unions in acting both to counter and accommodate the one-way street of company-centred ideologies. It is clear that there are sufficient grounds for arguing that the 'Nissan Way' is successful as a result of special contingent factors. We have elucidated many of these already, but one of the crucial variables of success is the ability to reach out to employees with the promise of achievement and dignity. However, this is only part of the story, for management success requires that this be replicated day in, day out. To make this happen, Nissan has had to ensure that the terms of employee fulfilment be predictable and, of course, this demands that individual workers are 'fulfilled' on company terms. This constraint is a significant feature of the management system itself. It requires two elements: an organisational framework which can ensure that the whole Nissan view of the world can be reproduced every day in every way (which is what teamworking for consensus is all about), and a veritable set of ideological practices which confirm this organisational framework.

What we are witnessing at Nissan is not only an organisation which depends upon and promotes consensus-building structures for quality products. The flipside of this is an organisational hierarchy of constraint, one that allows only those views of work which are commensurate with its own. By any terms of reference, this is in practice a disempowering, rather than an empowering, situation. What we are describing is a regime of subordination. Because of those socio-economic and local political factors described above, we feel we are accounting for what can best be described as a new regime of subordination. This is the bitter irony, the downside, of the exciting new 'Nissan Way', and it stands at the heart of the Nissan enigma.

Behind the cheerful appearance of equanimity and fulfilment lies another, disquieting reality—the New Regime of Subordination (Figure 4).

NEW REGIME OF SUBORDINATION: TEAMWORK, SUBJECTIVITY AND MANAGERIAL CONTROL

Teamworking, therefore, represents the social and organisational term for the constitution of relations of subordination, known as the 'Nissan Way', in workers' daily lives on the line. It is also, therefore, the necessary organisational form in which the legitimation of these relations of subordination can occur. This process of the legitimation of control works because team ideology succeeds where quality circles in the past have not. This is largely because the latter failed to extend company ideologies into the very identities of workers themselves (Doray, 1988).

Nissan's tripod of success

QUALITY   FLEXIBILITY   TEAMWORK

A *virtuous* circle depending upon consensus.
Teamworking is the social institution in which
this is made and remade anew each day.

New Regime of Subordination

CONTROL   EXPLOITATION   SURVEILLANCE

A *virtueless* circle derived from the operation of
Nissan's tripod.

Figure 4 The 'New Regime of Subordination' at Nissan.

Quality circles (QCs) are naturally limited in the extent to which they can assist management control. Historically, they arose out of the need to identify and contain the inefficiencies inherent in the operation of traditional mass-production systems (Parker, 1985). One problem for management has always been how to introduce the idea of quality into production proper. The drawback with QCs is that they fail to resolve the problem of quality-in-production because they require the temporary removal of employees from an inefficient system, forcing them to look at quality problems and their resolution, then putting them back into the old system again. Nevertheless, QCs can also be seen as an organisational attempt to talk directly to employees on management's terms (to the extent that unions are involved in QCs, the crucial issue for management is that QCs are seen as 'time out' of production where individuals can discuss technological matters in strictly neutral terms). Although the *kaizen* process at Nissan does achieve the latter, it differs markedly from QCs because it operates within a system of work organisation that is defined at every moment in the production cycle as a quest for quality. Everyone must think 'quality' in respect of the 'Nissan Way'. Each moment of the production process is checked for quality and quality must become second nature to all company employees. Improvement is to be a 'continuous process'. As ·Nissan itself makes clear: 'Kaizen may be applied anywhere, anytime, any-place. . . . Kaizen is not a suggestions scheme. If time and effort is spent in developing ideas for OTHERS to implement—nothing will happen! Kaizen IS improvement that can be achieved by ourselves' (Nissan, *Kaizen Leader Training Manual*, p. 1; original emphasis).

For management, it is also difficult to introduce quality into traditional mass-production systems because trade union ethics and craft pride often cut across management attempts to be the sole judge of quality. It is important to remember, therefore, that employee independence is sustained around autonomous trade unions. QCs can go so far in talking to workers directly where they are removed temporarily from production, but they cannot really tackle the problems of building in quality to the labour process. Neither can they eliminate the obstacle posed by autonomous unions to a one-dimensional managerial view of quality—back on the line, the union may be the judge of all good practice.

Other techniques are (and historically have been) used to elicit support, Measured Day Work being one example. But these are always bound to be hamstrung in that they too sit alongside independent trade union organisation and cannot guarantee delivery on a central aspect of control of labour in the way that Nissan's new regime of subordination can. The latter structures employee experience around the central tenets of its organisational imperative—quality for all time. Employees are controlled as they themselves control the quality process itself. This represents the key difference between the 'Nissan Way' and QCs. Where the latter took individuals out of production to show them a good idea about quality, the former, the 'Nissan Way', ensures that quality is built into the manufacturing process itself where the operation of each worker is measured by quality indicators (the VES—Vehicle Evaluation Score). *Pace* Littler's critique of labour process approaches which strive to identify the archetypal mechanism of organisational success (1982), we do not perceive the 'Nissan Way' as a management panacea for conflict. Nevertheless, few managements can claim Nissan's 'success'. Clearly, the configuration of success is also contingent on the local social and political relations defined in Chapters 1 and 2.

In respect of the internal aspect of this 'success', this can be attributed to the shifting of the locus of the control of workers onto workers themselves. The effect of this can be witnessed in the reinforcement of strong identities of personal independence which are typically central in the formation of people's subjectivities at work.

Many automotive manufacturers in the USA have operationalised teamworking, but it has to be recognised that even where the team concept exists within GM, Ford and Chrysler, the UAW, even though shackled by the current retreat of the labour movement, can still enact strong anti-company penalties. In fact, the only situation in the USA similar to our case is at Nissan's plant at Smyrna, Tennessee. Here, conditions are known to be subject to more criticism than at Nissan's Sunderland plant. It has been argued that at Smyrna, the presence of more rigid management practices is a salutary reminder of what can occur when there is no organised trade union: individuals at Smyrna find it extremely difficult to challenge management because of a particularly tight surveillance system.

This raises questions about the nature of the kind of international comparisons that can be made, and it is worth briefly considering the comparison with research in the USA, for our argument rests on a perception of NMUK as both unique and continuing an already existing series of strategic management options. This synthesis of practices established in the USA with adaptation to local circumstances in Britain provides for Nissan's uniqueness—its new regime of subordination. In pressing this point, we are going beyond the management-by-stress thesis advanced by Parker and Slaughter to account for the character and style of Japanese management practices in North-East England as opposed to the USA.

To recall, in their analysis of management-by-stress Parker and Slaughter refer to the ideal management system, which is one employing the team concept. They are primarily concerned with accounting for how this operates; however, this misses a more integrated view of the role of subjectivity and consciousness in subordination which would lead to a clearer understanding of how management-by-stress works. This rectification is all the more urgent since the example cited by Parker and Slaughter is of NUMMI, where the UAW exerts a strong influence. We agree with their view of the UAW's role as being what they term 'cooperationist', rather than the more traditional and (for them) defensible, 'participationist'. We might quibble at this juncture over the nature of the distinction, but for the most part, in the cooperationist scenario, they are describing an industrial relations situation where the union has virtually conceded the rules over co-determination. Nevertheless, there are still important points where the union has power, not the least being their organisational and political autonomy from GM-Toyota. Nissan at Smyrna, Tennessee, which Parker and Slaughter see as a further and more developed example of management-by-stress, bears closer comparison to our own study.

The point about management-by-stress is that it is seen to constitute the quintessential use by management of the team concept strategy. Parker and Slaughter see it as a totally integrated management system combining:

1) Speedup—ways for workers to do more work in less time.
2) 'Just-In-Time' (JIT) organisation of inventory and production.
3) Extensive use of outside contracting.
4) Technology designed to minimise indirect labour.
5) Design-for-manufacture products specifically designed to reduce labour costs.
6) Methods to reduce scrap.
7) Tighter management control.

(Parker and Slaughter, 1988, p. 16)

For Parker and Slaughter, management-by-stress contravenes all the accumulated logic and experience of a traditional management approach. This is indeed its intention. It is precisely by pinpointing weakness, creating breakdown, and stress-loading human and technological resources that 'weakness' can be perceived and dealt with. No need, with management-by-stress, to stockpile parts to guard against breakdown:

> Instead, the operating principle of management-by-stress is to systematically locate and remove such protections. The system, including its human elements, operates in a state of permanent stress. Stressing the system identifies both the weak points and those that are too strong. The weak points will break down when the stress becomes too much, indicating that additional resources are needed. Just as important, points that never break down are presumed to have too many resources, and are thus wasteful.

(ibid.)

This constant pressure of management-by-stress to seek out weak social and organisational links is a social power aspect of the utilisation of JIT inventory systems. These systems give too much possibility for resource disruption and, as was pointed out above, are extremely susceptible to both organised and unorganised social breakdown (Oliver and Wilkinson, 1988). Trade unions are one of the traditional power-brokers in auto plants and can be cited by management as a potential source of dislocation. Although Parker and Slaughter do not refer to this aspect of the presence of unions in this context, it is clearly one of those possible sources of 'breakdowns and glitches' (ibid.) for which management seek management-by-stress as a kind of pre-emptive strike.

The concept of management-by-stress is helpful, then, because it locates JIT in a broader framework of management control, thereby placing the issue of resource allocation firmly on the terrain of commitment to company goal attainment. However, as we argue below, it is impossible to explain commitment to work in terms of management-by-stress alone. It is relatively easy to control the operation of technical resources on the line, but not so straightforward where human labour is concerned. It is ultimately because of the unpredictability of human effort (despite Frederick Taylor) that management-by-stress is essential in order for JIT to work. Even if Nissan did not see independent trade unions as inimical to its work philosophy, it would still worry about them because of the need to ensure total control of the manufacturing operation, as dictated by JIT. Of course, as numerous examples from both the USA and Britain show, unions and management-by-stress can coexist. However, this typically derives from an environment where unions predate the introduction of the strategy. To this extent, we would agree with Parker and Slaughter that unions supporting management have often given up the fight. Nevertheless, it is not as straightforward as this, as the history of union and management opposition and negotiation at Ford UK testifies.

LIMITS TO THE MANAGEMENT-BY-STRESS ARGUMENT

There are other reasons for the opposition to independent unions at Nissan, and recognition of this leads us to consider some of the limitations of the management-by-stress argument. The latter tells us why and part of the 'how', as it were, of the link between JIT, teamwork and the role of quality in management practices. It has the additional benefit of explaining the rationality of the apparently irrational pressurising of human and technical resources to their very limits. This said, it is still vital to point out that the benefits for management of management-by-stress are that it devolves decisions downwards, while in addition individualising/personalising production problems, where line workers are encouraged to assume personal responsibility for difficulties. Nissan, unlike NUMMI and the other new production facilities in the USA, in practice put little time into counselling—though in theory much is made of its importance. At Nissan people are encouraged to view work problems as personal issues about which the company can do little. In a situation where unions can be incorporated, it matters little that they may be notionally independent so long as they withhold from challenging company philosophy, especially where it is the custom to delegate responsibility for error downwards. People need to build identities at work (including ones centred on the idea of responsibility), and from the company's standpoint, the less oppositional these are the better. With an entirely compliant union, they have no difficulty asserting their nostrums. At Nissan, one finds a strong ideological framework which creates precisely the sense of purpose needed for organisational survival. Management-by-stress needs commitment like no other management system ever has! Why would people work so hard otherwise? A strong company-centred philosophy is vital—at Nissan, teamworking provides the *institutional* imperative for the success of management-by-stress.

All of this continues to beg the question of 'how' the system prevails. In other words, what is the system of legitimacy that allows people not just to be pushed to and beyond the limit, but actually to take responsibility for the failures of the system? This is what Antonio Gramsci termed the pursuit of the hegemonic principle (Gramsci, 1971). How is it that men and women go along with, and in many ways actively and willingly participate in, the terms and conditions of their own subordination?

Operating a management-by-stress strategy in an automobile manufacturing plant leads to breakdowns, that necessary indicator of resource allocation demands within the system. A requirement of a management-by-stress approach is an absence of countervailing trade union organisation. What substitutes for the identity this can bestow is a strong corporate consciousness. It is also a corollary where social and technical integration require an ideology of company centred-ness, free from any potential social–political disruption. In the absence of strong trade union or overtly oppositional class identities of the kind that see the company philosophy as antithetical to any real pursuit of human dignity, the corporate consciousness prevails. Even if it is not the only consciousness, it hardly matters since there is no *social* space for counter-ideologies of a collectivist and solidaristic kind. As Knights and Willmott (1989) argue, the workplace provides for more than simply the possibility of class identities. At Nissan, identities of gender and place, for example, have a predominantly incorporationist bias. This reinforces insecurity, even where it does not clearly support company beliefs.

Yet it is true that the subjectivities people create at work mediate all sorts of antagonisms which at different times can provide the basis for disruption (as the interview above with Joe made clear—see p. 92—and as we illustrate further in Chapter 5 below, notably in our interview with Tim from 'final trim and chassis'). However, in the case of Nissan, we are concerned with how these identities, which are often forged out of insecurities, provide the basis for the success of the company's management strategy. The very real insecurities that fear of social isolation, or personal failure, can create, for example, lend a good deal of credibility to those sets of assimilative strategies which can form the framework for subjectivities. As Tony (see p. 129) points out: 'The lads have got families and mortgages.' And for those who do not, Colin's fear hit upon a more telling insecurity when he asked: 'Why be a martyr and get yourself a bad name for being like, big mister union man?' These assimilative strategies succeed because they attempt to provide feelings of togetherness on the back of a new corporate zeal. As Jimmy (above, p. 93) pointed out, the great virtue of Nissan is what he described as the 'family thing'. Part of our argument is that this is a necessary consequence of what is a fiercely competitive and tough work regime. The identities Nissan hopes to provide for its employees offer a welcoming homeliness. But beneath this welcome there is another imperative: the offer is clear—put up or shut up. But in a region of historically high levels of unemployment there is no real choice in practice.

As Knights and Willmott (1989) point out, such identities are indeed very real and cannot be thought of merely in terms of their compensatory character. But in another sense, as they themselves make clear, the subjectivities made in the workplace ensure, for the most part, a substantial degree of disempowerment. This finds an echo in John's criticism of a team meeting (p. 124). Even in their 'positive' guise, these identities can be limiting, although, as we highlight in the next chapter, strong personal commitments which can derive from external influences, as well as feelings of comradeship in work, do pose difficulties for the organisation (Joe—p. 92—makes this clear in his statement about the importance of trade unionism). But a crucial thing is their disabling impact in terms of excluding any collectivist consciousness that might identify with trade unionism. Quite apart from the fact that the dominant relations are disabling, we must also look to those relations which aim to ensure that this disablement and disempowerment can be delivered on a consistent basis.

From a management viewpoint, it is not enough that independent unions cease to function, for there is no guarantee that this will continue to be the case, or that commitment will be a necessary part of everyone's daily work experience. Nissan's regime of subordination is testament to this, for it requires that a new corporate worker identity will be created or at least that the scope for opposition will be squeezed out of the system. Although we cannot say that all identities created at work will be class identities, we need to be able to recognise that the structures that companies put up to define the contours of all aspects of employee subjectivity inhibit any sort of opposition. Historically, the main collective identity which challenges the managerial prerogative is that of class, in its many guises—though of course, as feminist research has pointed out, it would be unusual for class identity to occur in oppositional situations on its own (Westwood, 1984). By the same token it is clear that solidaristic experiences can often undermine other empowering identities, for example of gender (Cockburn, 1983).

Without doubt, organised and independent trade unions do not always resolve the problem of disempowerment at work. Nevertheless, because they can be independent of the company, they largely provide for the site of an alternative centre of empowerment—at the very least, in the work situation itself. If it was for this reason alone, Nissan would find it sufficient to worry about alternative loci of power, which is what alternative ideologies are all about. As we have seen, the identity Nissan provides is an identity for the whole person. While this can seek to exclude individual anxiety, as for many it does, it cannot take away the fear of job loss. Joan (above, p. 106), while speaking of the role of quality control in highlighting individual error, also told us that one of her great motivators was the fear of unemployment. The Nissan work situation, then, is best characterised as one in which a strong paternalistic management structure indulges those who are prepared to take sustenance from it. To this extent, individual fear of social and personal isolation can be assuaged in so far as one accepts the system. It is not as if there is an alternative—there is not; and for precisely those local social, economic and political factors outlined in Chapter 1, the firm's youthful workers are hardly predisposed to consider one . . . yet (the average age of the assembly-line work-force in 1989 was 27).

For sure, these subjectivities created in the workplace are another part of the constituted terrain of subordination, and the structure of the management system, as we have described it, continues this for it channels personal insecurity into the caring arms of the 'Nissan Way' (teamwork, quality, flexibility, *kaizen*). While personal insecurity is seemingly provided for, personnel subordination is assured. In this very real sense, a search for security at work for one's own identity becomes a terrible trap of enslavement. An employee's need for a secure identity is turned against him or her self.

This is the crucial way in which we can begin to unravel one of the main paradoxes of a management-by-stress influenced system:

> the characteristic response under management-by-stress is . . . pressure is allowed to transmit through to production workers, team leaders and lowest level management by making *them* solve the problem and catch up. There is no external assistance until management is satisfied that extraordinary efforts and all the resources available to the team have been used.

> (Parker and Slaughter, 1988, pp. 17–18)

That employees not only allow this system to prevail, but seek to maintain it, suggests that ideology is as important an influence as coercion, or merely passivity, in the face of the great monolith. Although many employees we interviewed felt that a challenge to the company's ideology was at present unfeasible, through a mixture of the nature of the local labour market and their own particular social and personal commitments, others like Jimmy, who spoke of the importance of the company's family ethos, expressed a willingness to engage in the Nissan rhetoric of togetherness. In so doing, we need to repeat that what they are express-ing commitment to is an ideological system at once disempowering, but which offers the space for personal power and a form of solidarism which in traditional plants is offered by independent trade unions. The solidarism is provided for where the experience of collective effort on the line is articulated in terms of those caring relations, which are so redolent of familial security and dependability, as accounted for previously.

Nevertheless, the individualism and solidarism of the 'Nissan Way', refracted as they are through canons of corporate identity, cannot exclude the consciousness of fear and personal turmoil that extends from the experience of the physical harshness of line work. It is well to remember that others can have a sense of solidarism which is antipathetic to the 'Nissan Way'. For these workers, the corporate ethos has a different import; in the team wonderland, when they do not agree, they experience personal isolation; in the Company Council and the paternalistic structure of the organisation, they are socially isolated and politically excluded. The Company Council comprises 50% management nominees and 50% elected representatives from the workforce. There is no guarantee that either the appointees or the representatives will be union members. Joe (p. 93) felt the Company Council was a 'complete shambles', while Rob, a technician, said he felt it was irrelevant to any grievance he might have. For him, the problem lies with the nature of the system of election and in the fact that it is 'basically a rubber stamp affair for Nissan's views'. Because it can operate as a form of patronage, representatives are in his view unlikely ever to raise issues that might be deemed unpopular by the company.

For workers who find the 'Nissan Way' unconvincing, life at Nissan is different. Rather than being exceptions to the rule, their brave testimony serves as a reminder of the object of the 'Nissan Way'. Nissan's response has always been that if they do not like it they can go elsewhere. It is precisely because the company cannot tolerate dissent that people are often forced out. When they do stay, it is often to do with the slackness of the local external labour market. Those who accept the 'Nissan Way' have no recourse to an independent organisation that might support their interests independently of the company. When employees do criticise the company, they find their criticisms are lost in the great wave of company views of life. There is no group with the cohesion of Nissan which is capable of providing a sufficiently powerful counterview of the world. Because there is no alternative source of interpretation, there is no language in which grievances might be expressed. In the next chapter we address the tensions that are nevertheless inherent in this industrial relations context.

Chapter 5: **Working the 'Nissan Way'**

The new regime of subordination depends upon the careful management of internal and external resources. These include: the control of land and the social space created by the local consensus in favour of the company; a new labour force; an internal regime which requires consent for production; a compliant union. In the preceding chapters we have elaborated upon these critical variables. At the same time, we argued that these cannot exclude social and psychological conflict at work. We argued that although organised and unorganised counterviews are by definition excluded there is another crucial point to be made.

Although this exclusion can work (for the present) in respect of structural determinants of change it becomes more problematic in relation to individual and unorganised personal responses to the reality of assembly-line work. As Knights and Willmott (1989) argue, the search for secure identities forged in the workplace is double-edged. We make the point that at Nissan the way individuals react to the insecurities of life on the line can help to constitute the integrity needed for consensus. This derives from the one certainty employees have, which is that work provides for a sense of security—until or unless this goes unrewarded. These elements of security, which are engendered out of success in competition with others, can lead to personal disquiet and unhappiness. In the event of the latter there are few buttresses of support. At the same time, identities created at work depend upon, as they reinforce, external and already existing views of life (Westwood, 1984). Many of these extra-company views prevail in the creation and reconstitution of life at work where, for many, the bottom line is that Nissan is an employer of labour in a competitive world. For those who feel disillusioned and isolated, they either continue because they lack any alternative employment or they leave. Some do leave Nissan after difficult deliberation.

For those who do stay in spite of their many grievances there are a limited number of options. One is to internalise the problems and disagreements but to keep quiet about them, which as we have pointed out is one of the functions of the overall management strategy, which seeks to personalise employee responses to difficulties experienced at work. Another response is to internalise, as in the first case, but to discuss these difficulties with team leaders and supervisors. A drawback here is that team meetings last for about ten minutes before production begins and are mostly taken up with routine issues arising from the previous day's work. The final possible response is to discuss issues with trusted colleagues in dinner breaks, but these are informal and are outside the normal institutional context. However, the drawback with all these strategies is that discontent continues to mount up, and where it does create difficulties on the line people are treated less than sympathetically.

There are many employees at Nissan who feel so aggrieved and it is to them that we now turn. Their voices of everyday dissent have never been heard before because the company indirectly discourages them from voicing their disquiet not only, as we have demonstrated, inside the organisation, but also, when it can, in public. They have all risked sanctions from their employer by speaking to us—in itself an indication of the crucial importance Nissan attaches to its closed world of insecurity, and as clear an example as one could wish of the imposed nature of its consensus. In addition, the following discussion derived from our in-depth interview material tells us just what the other side of the 'Nissan Way' means for those who work in the so-called post-Fordist world. It is to protect these employees that we have used pseudonyms. Even if some of their allegations are exaggerated, the fact that they have made them to us suggests that Nissan is not the happy family it claims to be.

AN ERA OF NEW WORK EXPERIENCE?

Idle minds are the devil's playthings

(Ford Manager, River Rouge plant, 1930)

You ask about Fordism/Post-Fordism. As far as I am concerned we are a Post-Fordist company

(Senior Nissan Manager, 1989)

In the context of this very tight production system, described by Slaughter (1987) as management-by-stress (MBS), we want to consider the character of employee responses to a work and organisational culture variously described as 'Japanised' or 'post-Fordist'. We now turn to some of our interview material under four headings: Management Practices and the Response of Workers; Work Intensity and Management-by-Stress; Worker Attitudes to Existing Unionism; and Limits and Horizons of Dissent. This puts into relief the problems associated with the way commentators and researchers consider the bipolarity of Fordism/post-Fordism, for it is clear that conflicts deriving from exploitation at the point of production are far from belonging to the distant past. These are no less conflicts about class, just because they are also conflicts about other identities. Nevertheless, there are many who, in spite of the individualising impact of the 'Nissan Way', have little difficulty perceiving themselves as workers on the line. Conflict at the point of production continues to produce class and individual conflicts in the so-called post-Fordist era.

Management practices: the response of workers

If we consider the question of managerial practices and the part they play in excluding or more properly excising conflict, and the efforts to which management goes in ensuring line discipline, it is very interesting how acutely aware line workers themselves are both of the role of line supervision and the structure of work organisation in maintaining cohesion and excluding work and company antipathy. As we illustrated in Chapters 3 and 4, this cohesion is achieved by fostering individualism via competitiveness and peer surveillance.

For example, Bill, who works as a spot-welder, emphasised the problems of the Neighbour Check System (NCS) and Vehicle Evaluation System (VES). These make it possible to trace faults to specific work teams and individuals on the line and to award a daily or weekly score to each operative. The NCS is both a way to ensure continuity and 'quality' along the line between teams, and a form of peer monitoring between workers. Bill was asked for his view of the VES:

Bill: The way they score the VES system they would be looking for dirt on the job or to see if there was any shavings coming off that would prove that the tip of the gun hadn't been dressed properly; what you'd get is an offshoot of work which is razor sharp, particularly if it was in the engine compartment—what they say is the future owner could slice his finger open on it. They check all sorts of things on the car, to make sure the bodywork on the door is flush, etc.

Q: Is this worked out later to give you an achievement score?

Bill: Yes, there are graphs on the door outside of the meeting room—this is the QCV board—quality, cost and volume, something like that, and it shows you graphs on the quality—it's amazing really.

Q: Can this be traced back to an individual?

Bill: Well, yes, each body is numbered and they know which shift it's been worked on and depending on which part of the car they can tell which team had done the job—but it depends because sometimes we change over so you can't really say which individual made a mistake, but they don't try to do this, they just say try to improve, keep an eye on it.

Not all respondents concur in this, as our reference to Joan (p. 106) illustrates. She, like others, was more critical of VES and NCS as a form of surveillance in ways that concur with our conceptual analysis of the role these variables play in safeguarding total quality management in the teamworking process. David, who worked for a large engineering company in Gateshead before being made redundant, echoed Joan's point:

David: As the car comes through sealer it goes through ED and sanding and [everyone has] a part of the car to do. So if a fault is on their quarter then management know that that bloke has missed it. So you always know where it has been missed—who did the car.

Let us return to Bill for the present.

Q: So if you get material in and it's defective do you indicate that to your supervisor or do you just get on and do your job?

Bill: If you can do it yourself you do it, for example if it is light rust then you can do it yourself—it then goes through an ED dip which uses electro-currents. We used to have a repair area—two or three lads who used to be permanent and they used to repair it for you.

Bill believed that this led to a form of 'sniping', as he called it, on colleagues, which confirmed the attitude of management. Nissan itself speaks of the Neighbour Check System as a system that provides for employee peer surveillance. The interesting thing is that in spite of this, Bill still considers he and some of his mates have not been incorporated by the company:

Q: Is Nissan's company image about being part of a 'family' evident?

Bill: Well, I think they probably realise that where we work it is quite bolshie anyway you know.

Q: What do you mean 'quite bolshie'?

Bill: Well we don't toe the company line and there are some people who wouldn't say a word against Nissan but we are pretty anti-Nissan really.

Yet this feeling of independence can be difficult to achieve where management employs sanctions. These are often invoked and enforced in the technical operation of the assembly-line itself. According to John, behaviour is defined and sanctioned through bureaucratic channels, as are individual responses to work issues of both a social and a technical nature. These channels are the team meetings, which legitimise team leader authority relations. Problems are sometimes dealt with *in situ*, others are highlighted afterwards in team meetings. Take this account of management attitudes to carrying out work tasks at variance with management-defined procedures:

Q: Was anybody ever pulled up for not doing the job properly?

John: Yes.

Q: In what kind of way, can you describe what happened?

John: On the morning we used to have a meeting—just our group, ten lads—and we'd sit in a circle and if you'd done anything wrong you got put in the middle and shouted at—'You've done this wrong'. There are lads of 35 years old who would be shouted at by lads who were team leaders of 22 years old.

Q: So not just questioned or talked to, they got shouted at?

John: Yes.

Q: What else happened in the team meetings?

John: They told us if there was any news—they discussed how the production the day before had gone—if they got the target, if we reached the standards and what targets they wanted to achieve, things like that.

Q: Did you say anything back?

John: Everybody just kept quiet because the supervisors were never wrong! Doesn't matter even if you were right—in their eyes you were always wrong.

Q: Can you give me an example of such a situation?

John: Well, they tried to tell us to do things in a different way—and we did it that way for a day and the target at the end of the day was worse and then the next day we went back to our methods and the target was better and yet they still said it was us to blame, saying we must have been pressing on too hard with the 'tack cloth' and not concentrating enough.

Q: So they were critical of both quality and output—even though the way you did things was better?

John: Yes, it was the supervisor who said it had to be done his way.

Q: What were the other lads' attitudes to this?

John: The lads listen and just take it in and did not say anything. If they thought it was wrong they just talked about it at tea break. I think the supervisors—the management—had all the power.

This assumed subservience to a logic of production is carried over into line-training and suggests an experience of work not dissimilar to a work situation traditionally perceived as Fordist. This identity with Fordist work experiences was reflected above all in the rhythm and tempo of work, and in the casual character of line training. John's views on learning the job suggest an interesting variance with the ethos of NCS.

Q: Did you work on the same part of the line all the time?

John: Yes.

Q: What kind of training did you get apart from the days watching the other lads?

John: None, you just have to teach yourself after that—you get told if a job is dirty that you have been pressing on with your 'tack cloth' too hard and getting fibres on the job. They didn't go around and show you.

Q: What about the group of lads you were working with. Did they help you, did they show you how to do things?

John: Well it was not like a group, everybody had their own individual job to do; as long as your job was OK it did not matter what your mate was doing as long as yours was all right. The way I looked at it everybody just looked after themselves; as long as your mate's job was all right he was not bothered about yours.

Work intensity and management-by-stress

This pressure towards self-preservation was itself an element in allowing the intensity of work to increase:

Q: What happened if, for example, you had to to to the toilet?

John: No chance. Unless you waited for the break.

Q: There was no cover, no one to step in and help you out?

John: Sometimes the supervisor but very rarely; he was always watching the machines further up the line.

Q: In terms of the work itself, how intense was it physically?

John: At some stages it was hard—in the summer when there was a lot of cars to do then the line would be speeded up; sometimes when it was cooling off a bit the line got turned down though. Sometimes we would do 350 cars a day, sometimes 300 or 250.

Q: How did you feel after a day's work?

John: Shattered. Especially because we in the paint shop had to tidy up after we had done a day's work—in the paint shop that was another hour, working with a bucket of thinners.

Along the same lines, our earlier respondent Bill was asked:

Q: You're trained to do your own basic maintenance work?

Bill: You're trained to do your own maintenance—but if you need maintenance workers they will come running. You learn this in your own area but if you are good enough they will put you anywhere.

Q: What do you mean 'good enough'?

Bill: Well, if you can do this job in a standard time obviously this is the same speed as the line; you have got to get the parts to the next section or whatever; it's not as overpowering as it seems because we are lucky; some of us can do the job in less than the standard time and we can build the stock up and we can do other things like help somebody else.

Q: So does standard time change? Has it got quite fast?

Bill: Oh yes! it's incredible.

Q: Has it increased in line with higher production quotas?

Bill: Well it has been brought in to meet the production quota, but it's also been brought in gradually of course. What they do is they give you a number on a certain day and we all say 'we'll never do that'; but you can, it's incredible how you can do it. They have brought in extra men as well. When I first started there was only one man on my job—on two jigs.

Q: So there is no idle time?

Bill: Well you can get it if you want it, but you've got to think of your mates as well and help them out; but they have got it down so there is not much idle time. On day shift the break is at 10 a.m. for 15 minutes then again at a quarter-to-three to 3 p.m. That is apart from dinner—apart from that I do checks on the spot welding every now and then.

Q: Are you tired at the end of the day?

Bill: Oh yes, for me it's very tiring!

Q: Do you worry about having to do that day in and day out?

Bill: Not anymore; I've got used to it and most of the lads just accept it—you do get days when we've a spare man; at least we should have one but most of the time he's moved on to the Liger line to fill in because they have a lot of trouble with lads off sick. [Liger line is company jargon for marrying power train to body shell.]

At this point in the interview, Bill's wife interjected:

Muriel: I hate Nissan for what they have done to him.

Q: What do you mean?

Muriel: Well, because he's so tired and he has lost 1½ stone in the time he has been there. I remember when he first started he was falling asleep over his meal on an evening; he used to say 'there is something I really want to watch on TV', but he would always fall asleep before the end.

Another respondent, Alan, was asked about the stress of working with minimal idle time:

Q: The day shift comes at six, so you have got two shifts in the factory over-lapping? Do you get a chance to see the other shift?

Alan: No, it's not like that. When your shift is over you may have a breakdown of a part and the shift that is coming on, say at ten to six, are having a cup of tea and they have to get out; they are not allowed to sit about chatting or anything like that; I mean that is how you would normally hand over to another shift, have a bit of a chat saying 'well this broke down, that broke down', but one shift has to scarper.

It is clear from our respondents' experiences that management's policy is to keep the pressure on the workforce in order to maintain production levels. This was also the experience of a supervisor whom we interviewed:

Q: So you are in the factory for half an hour and you are not actually in charge of what is going on and the other shift has taken over?

Supervisor A: When things are pretty quiet you are supposed to be out monitoring line watch; you are not supposed to just sit down and put your feet up, but you can walk about and have a bit of a chat; you're supposed to look active all the time.

Q: Is that the only chance you get to talk to other people?

Supervisor A: Well, that is about the only time—you very rarely get a chance to discuss things with the production line—they just have not got time; they are just going at it hammer and tongs.

Over the last twelve months, working pressures have increased as Nissan raised production levels. Alan was asked about the effects felt on the production line:

Q: Has the pace of your work increased as the pace of production has increased?

Alan: Yeah, it has, yes.

Q: Do you find this stressful?

Alan: Yeah, it does sicken you off a bit. Well when I come back home all I want to do is put my feet up; there is much frenzy caused when a machine breaks down; you have got to get there quick and that is the main bit of physical exertion and getting filthy dirty; and when that is over you have to go straight back out again checking so you never get a chance to rest; even when you are having your break the telephone goes and it's 'Oh no, here we go again', you know.

Q: There is no question of saying 'Well, I am going to finish my dinner first'?

Alan: Oh there is, yeah, you know every now and again you say that, but in the end you always go out, you always do. The thing is what should happen really is the Supervisor should say, well an electrician and a fitter can have their bait now while the other two are still on patrol and then the other two can come in. I think that would do, whereas you have not got the atmosphere to sit and talk.

It is clear that the new, integrated (Just-In-Time) production cycles do not present an unambiguously different experience of assembly-line work. Customised production, a supposed feature of flexible manufacturing systems, leads neither to up-skilling nor to a significantly enhanced experience of work. The comments of workers above could just as easily have been made by employees in the more traditional automotive plants so decried by Nissan and its company 'Way'.

Worker attitudes to existing trade unionism

Trade unions usually articulate organised alternative positions in an industrial setting, but at Nissan the union, the AEU, stays clear of this. In any event, with an initial membership of less than one in five, which has grown to less than one in three with management encouragement, it is in no position to foster an oppositional perspective. This business unionism or 'New Realist' view fits uncomfortably with the experiences of many of our interviewees. The response of shop-floor workers tells us much about everyday concerns of health and safety and something too of the feeling of impotence which is a result of the fact that many feel the union is irrelevant. It would be difficult for a union to stake a claim in anyone's concerns where it is irrelevant to their everyday fears.

Tony and Steve were asked about their attitudes to the union, their friends' predilections, and how the union helped with matters of health and safety. Their responses are revealing of the attitude to the AEU, which is after all the only (recognised) union. We began our discussion with Tony by asking whether the union could not have been called in to clear a health and safety issue.

Q: It never occurred to anybody that the union would be a way to deal with problems?

Tony: No one dared mention the union; they just got on with it so long as they had a job.

Q: Did it strike you as strange that people didn't talk about a union—car workers are usually well organised?

Tony: Lads have got mortgages and families—so, as long as they had a job they just put up with it.

Steve was also asked about health and safety matters and the social consequences of work practices on line workers:

Q: When you felt unhappy about some aspect of the work itself what did you do about it?

Steve: Every night I got thinners in my eyes—the machines are above you and you've just got a cloth; the thinners would just drip off the cloth.

Q: So this was not the type of thing you could talk about at a team meeting?

Steve: No.

Q: So who could you complain to?

Steve: It was rare anybody wanted to complain because the managers had so much power the lads didn't think it was worth it. The complaints were just what the lads talked about on the dinner time; they would take it out on each other.

Q: How do you mean 'take it out on each other'?

Steve: Talk about it with each other rather than let the supervisors hear them.

Q: But there is a union in Nissan?

Steve: A small union, yes.

Another interviewee, Simon, was asked for his feelings generally about the status of the AEU, company-sanctioned grievance procedures, and workers' feelings about the union. His attitude again is illustrative of the low regard held by the company for the union, and the clear signals received by workers that being a good trade unionist is not the route to a successful career.

Simon: I wouldn't work for a company without a union.

Q: Would you have considered yourself a trade unionist before working for Nissan?

Simon: I never really thought about it much until I worked there. I just gradually thought about it the longer I worked there . . . the union [outside the plant] is just one thing that is just not mentioned so far as the supervisors are concerned; neither in meetings or on the conference days we had to attend.

Q: And there was never anybody there from the union?

Simon: I couldn't tell you anybody who was in the union.

Eddie claims he was given the sack because 'his face did not fit'. He says he was never told why, and that his inability to find out has ensured his unemployability in the region.* We asked him whether he felt quite aggrieved by what Nissan has done to him:

Eddie: Yes.

Q: You said that many people have left the job because they have had enough.

Eddie: There are only two lads left who I worked with still there—all the rest have just packed the job in. There is a lad that I trained, he is still working there. I still go out with him on a Friday night, he keeps me up to date with what is happening. Some of the lads have just left to go back on the dole; I spoke to one of them.

Even the representatives from the Company Council need to be careful when it comes to indicating shop-floor views. We asked Derek if the Company Council gets involved in day-to-day things?

Derek: No, not that I know of.

Q: What do they do then?

Derek: They are just sitting on the fence; they are just part of the company—it is a company council—the representative comes and tells us what has been decided,

* We have no reason for believing this dismissal to have been unlawful.

what the company wants. He gets our viewpoints on it and then he goes back and supposedly gives our views on it.

Q: Was he elected by you?

Derek: I think he was, yeah, but apparently he can't speak up too loudly; they can't actually voice their heartfelt opinions, especially for our shop.

Q: Why is that?

Derek: Well, Nissan don't want to hear things like that, you know . . . besides it may reflect badly on him, you know, if he brings a bad opinion.

Q: So people are sensitive how things will reflect on their own team in terms of promotion and so on?

Derek: Yeah, generally people are pretty guarded about what they say.

Q: Are there any obvious cases of people who have a grievance because they are being somehow held back?

Eddie: Well, there are supposedly channels for dealing with things like that, and say for instance training and things like that—that has been a big bugbear, that was one of the reasons this lad packed in because he had been told he would be going on a training course, but in two years he had not been on anything so it is always being raised as well.

Limits and horizons of dissent

The dissatisfaction and incipient dissent, a far cry from Nissan's New Age of post-Fordist bliss, has one safety valve—a high labour turnover of, on some estimates, 20%. The other way in which dissatisfaction is stymied is a management realism about the rigours of assembly-line toil (rhetoric about happy families aside) which suggests the need for a degree of sensitivity to the fact that conflict and antipathy need to be handled with great care. Management responses to dissatisfaction can sometimes tell us much—that antipathy to line tempo and work discipline is an endemic feature of hard industrial toil in this 'new age' as much as in 'former times'. This comes over clearly when workers talk of their disillusionment with the company, engendered by the reality, as against the rhetoric, of life at Nissan. Both management 'fear' of dissent, and worker disillusionment, are communicated very clearly in the following interviews with two workers from 'final trim and chassis'. In addition, these interviews also reveal a deep undercurrent of resentment towards the company which was felt by many of those to whom we spoke, and it offers the potential that workers' struggles in the future are not impossible.

Tim said he was 'disillusioned' with Nissan.

Q: When you say disillusioned do you mean that some people went in with the notion that Nissan may represent something new?

Tim: Yeah.

Q: In what way?

Tim: Well, I think they thought it would be a modern factory and a management who had an idea of what they were doing, whereas it is just not that way at all.

Q: Is management not what you thought then?

Tim: Oh yeah! It's certainly not what I was expecting because I have been to Japan and there they really get things done, but at Nissan it is the same as anywhere else.

Q: It makes you wonder what will happen when production really steps up if people are disillusioned now. What do you envisage happening in the future?

Tim: Oh, within about four or five years you are going to have a strike. It will happen because people realise that there is nothing special about the place really; and in the end people will just say 'Oh, stuff it' and people will just go on strike.

Q: Do you think that is likely to happen?

Tim: I think it will, yeah.

Q: You say you think it will happen but if what you describe as a high turnover (about 20%) is accurate, does that not work as a kind of safety valve?

Harry, who also works on final trim and assembly, interjected at this point:

Harry: It possibly could, yeah, but the lad that left just last week apparently he had quite a few words to say about why he was leaving, you know, and previous to that he had been there since the company started as well. What I would like to say now may lead people back to me. . . .

Q: Well don't say it then . . .

Harry: But I would like to say something quite pertinent about morale—this was not last week, this was the week before the lad left, we had all hit a pretty bad morning—I forget what it was about—but anyway the supervisor was going to come and see us and try and find out why things had hit a low. On the Monday there was this lad came in with a resignation so that was another weight on his mind. And what happened then was the supervisor gets the senior supervisor in to ask the lad why he was leaving, and everything, and he gave him a good mouthful about why he was leaving; and the senior supervisor obviously gave the Nissan viewpoint. Anyway, it must have been reasonably amicable the way they parted like—there wasn't a fist fight or anything like that. But all the problems about morale the week before were forgotten, because this lad had left and that's it, you know, it has all just been forgotten. The whole thing about morale though is it bubbles up every now and again and then they are pressed back down, but the next time it comes up I think it is even worse.

It is important that we contextualise these articulated experiences of workers in the current debates about the meaning of new working practices. They indicate a series of work experiences which are not particularly novel. It is also important to note that numerous interviewees revelled in the experience of 'group work' on the line in the form of team-centred production units. Several were enthusiastic in their commitment to this kind of assembly-line work. One team leader, Jack, helped us interpret teamwork as surveillance and corporativist subordination when he said:

Jack: The team helps us all over difficult patches. You help me when it goes tough—I scratch your back kind of thing. You watch out for me and I watch out for you.

This encapsulates the double-edged nature of teamwork in the context of 'Just-In-Time'. It makes intense assembly-line work more sustainable. Individuals are linked together by a common sense of team spirit, which for the company looks like company centredness but which for employees is a good basis for survival in a tough and hostile industrial landscape. In any case, it is not a question of management believing their own rhetoric. Even if management were to forgo this rationalisation of teamwork, its central role in ensuring continuity of production would not cease. Most workers said two things about teamwork, sometimes holding both views at the same time: that it was good and that it was a sham. The important and interesting point for research is that when pressed they said that 'good for us' meant the same as 'good for the company'. As Harry said, it is a 'more civilised way to work'. In other words, teamwork helped workers to survive in a tough industrial world.

CONCLUSION

What this set of attitudes tells us about interpretations of working environments is important. It is not enough, if and where people want to challenge something, that they do so individually. Many of our sources, as well as those quoted here, have clearly disdained the way Nissan works and felt grievances at many different levels. What they lack is a series of sustainable alternative views of work which have currency and, therefore, legitimacy among many people within and between different teams. The conventional mechanism for achieving this is a functioning, autonomous trade union or unions. In the absence of this, the company makes all the running when it comes to providing collective opinions about the nature of the world.

Chapter 6: **Conclusions**

The North-East of England is said by many commentators to be at the centre of
the industrial transformation currently sweeping the UK's national economy. We
began the inquiry into one company's role in this sea of change by declaring our
interest in the people who work in the auto industry. While this focus meant
steering clear of assessing the outcome of market liberalism and Thatcherite
policies in overall terms for the UK economy, it allowed concentration on the
substance of the claims made for an industrial transformation. Social science
theorists often remain locked in the contradictions and lacunae of theoretical
disputes, but our focus on a single company in one local economy offers a degree of
empirical evidence essential to taking the theoretical debates further. What, then,
has emerged from this investigation?

   In the first instance, as we discussed in Chapter 1, there is a growing globalisa-
tion of manufacturing activity and ownership, as represented in the auto industry.
In the second place, and just as vividly for our purposes, the evidence is of a local-
isation in the effects of these macroeconomic phenomena. The immediate events
in a given local economy—in this case Sunderland's—prove to have their origins
not just in the corporate headquarters of a foreign multinational, but at a level
which transcends the locality and even the nation state. Japanese auto firms are
now the only genuinely global ones in the sense that their volume production platforms operate in each of the three major world markets for motor vehicles (Japan,
the USA and Europe). The decision-making power now established in the hands
of these titans of late-twentieth-century capitalism can make or break notions of
local, or even national, political independence in the matter of economic
regeneration. For specific evaluation of the consequences of this concentration of

ownership of production, and hence domination of markets, critical social science must now turn on a case-by-case basis to places like Sunderland.

The evidence from our study of Sunderland's experience of courting and winning the Nissan investment provides little comfort for the view that constructive economic regeneration can be planned and managed by state intervention. The 1980s witnessed the onset of government policies to restructure British industry via an alternative mode of intervention. This was a mode in which the state intervened to privatise or run down nationally owned sectors of the economy. At the same time, fiscal policy saw to it that unemployment was the main weapon against inflation, turning the British economy into an attractive proposition for foreign capital in search of cheap labour from amongst the growing numbers of the country's unemployed. Backing up this far-reaching and often radical programme of market liberalism has been the Thatcher governments' consistent denigration of organised labour for its role in the failed tripartism or corporatism which used to plan the economy in previous decades. As a result Britain now boasts the most stringent anti-union laws in the EC and, as we have argued, such circumstances constitute a significant attraction for investment by Japanese private capital in the UK.

At the level of the Sunderland local economy the evidence is that corporate power experiences few obstacles when what is on offer is employment creation of a significant magnitude. In Chapter 2 we concluded not only that the company's access to cheap and plentiful resources of land and labour was the determining factor in its choosing one locality from the many on offer, but also that the local economy should not expect much else in return when the bargain was struck. This is because the terms are set according to the priorities of the incoming investor, as the senior partner to the contract, and thus the provider of work and bearer of gifts. Little is made of the obvious public contribution to this exercise in the form of regional development grants and selective financial assistance, since in Thatcher's Britain—even in a place with Sunderland's historical strength of Labour support—at least the appearance of the enterprise culture must rule the day. Despite the public relations gloss put on this, however, there is no mistaking the reality that the Nissan investment remains a shared-risk undertaking between private capital and the state to provide work in a depressed region which is already the victim of the branch plant economy syndrome. In this sense, not much has changed.

The integrated production systems used by Japanese auto firms offer new employment opportunities when transplanted to a depressed area like Sunderland. Nevertheless, the argument we put forward is once again sceptical of the claims, and doubtful about the evidence that regeneration of the local economy as a whole is now on the cards. The skills relevant to making cars, as opposed to, say, ships, are heavily company-specific. Whereas in Sunderland's past there were several diverse companies in shipbuilding, and the skills were transferable across other aspects of heavy engineering in the area, this is not true of auto manufacturing. Sunderland now possesses one major firm in this sector, Nissan, and in the absence of a diverse and extensive automotive industry—as in, say, Coventry —the characterisation of skills learnt at Nissan as 'company-specific' remains fair. In addition, there is little reassurance in the experience of the US auto industry. As we have discussed, the transplanting from Japan not just of the final vehicle manufacturer but also of components suppliers, questions the view that indigenous sectors of the British auto industry—whether in the Sunderland area, or elsewhere—are receiving a positive stimulus. In fact the reverse may be about to happen, so that the Thatcherite era in economic policy-making will be regarded as having sealed the fate of the indigenous British auto industry as a major contributor to the economy, both as the main provider for UK-based firms and as an exporting success. This may turn out to be true not just for the motor vehicle manufacturers themselves—most of them owned by US or European parent firms —but also for the existing British components industry.

Our purpose in introducing these issues in the early chapters of the book was not just to record a critical perspective on the political handling of Britain's economic prospects. The full consequences of the transplanting of Japanese auto production systems in the UK economy will not be fully realised until the middle or the end of the 1990s. However, this critical perspective aside, there was another reason for first exploring the components of Japanese production systems and the subsequent domination of the Sunderland local economy by Nissan. The sort of external environment created in the local and national economy by these events is directly linked to the imperatives of the company's internal environment.

The external environment has seen an emphasis on market liberalism and private-sector remedies for economic problems: the withdrawal of state support from the North-East's nationalised industries—mainstays of the local economy; the resulting levels of local and regional unemployment—becoming the highest in England; and the persistence of radical anti-union legislation. Characteristically, public statements about this environment engage in a deliberate practice of reconstructing reality, so that, for example, Nissan was applauded as a pathbreaking winner for the private sector, conveniently ignoring public subsidies, while unionbusting laws were misrepresented as the means for liberating the individual. We find this same resort to reconstruction of the real world when we turn to the internal environment at Nissan.

Nissan managers and company literature describe their world in terms usually geared towards convincing us that the old world has passed on. The language is rhetorical and conveniently suggestive of the negative attitudes the present has left behind. The rhetoric encompassing Nissan's harmonious world view and working relations has to be more than coincidental. All the words in the lexicon exude harmony, realism and sensitivity (for those at work) and caring (for those who buy the products). In the analysis in Chapters 3 and 4, we focused on four recurring themes, which together constitute the 'Nissan Way': flexibility, consensus, teamwork and quality. The first three of these relate to a quest for harmony which sounds almost arcadian in its commitment to honest, decent work. There are no employers and employees in this world, just the Nissan family of high achievers.

This family of achievers cares for the people, all of us, who are tempted to buy or who own the family's products. Who would think of mistrusting a decent, hard-working family?

'Flexibility' in the Nissan lexicon means that those at work must get the goods ready for our individual needs on time. 'Consensus' refers to the need for the family team to be in agreement, and where dissent is allowed this is best worked out between the caring and committed relatives (keep it in the family!). 'Team-work' means that we can all achieve together since there are no essentially different views of the world. Starting from here, it becomes clear that differences are not a matter of principle, but of variations on a theme. According to the Fordist scenario, solidarity develops on the line as a consequence of an immediacy of similar work experience. Representatives from unions reinforce, at a cultural level, the negative view of this experience where work is owned by someone else (not one of us), who must offer suitable remuneration for alienating work. People do not experience their work in an ideological vacuum. Historically, corporate organisations such as unions were created to protect people from the rigours and one-dimensional experience of assembly-line work. Where unions are weak, or absent, typical company ideologies interpret line work in simplistic terms of the Human Relations school of management. This school of thought assumes that industrial relations problems derive from employee ignorance of management aims.

Nissan has developed this further by creating dedicated practices for company-specific tasks in assembly-line work. These require worker participation constituted in such a way as to reinforce the consensual rhetoric at an ideological level. By this strategy, workers implicate themselves by participation in discipline. In fact, by disciplining others when pointing out faults, they discipline themselves. In such a way, a whole system of self-subordination begins to develop. Finally, 'quality' means the customer comes first if the family's reputation is to be maintained. The Neighbour Check system, QCV, and VES are the mechanisms for helping your neighbour/brother develop his potential to build in quality. These totemic emblems define a brave new world of company-centred idealism set against the conflict of an old worn-out regime that we might just call 'Fordist'.

So it would seem that at Nissan, minds are no less idle and the Devil is kept just as much at bay: contented minds keep the Devil away . . . perhaps. But at Nissan the construction of an idea of contentment is an indispensable condition of organisational harmony and work intensification.

This brings us nearer to a more helpful view of post-Fordist claims. The important issue is that, however defined, Fordism is clearly characteristic of a certain period of capitalist production. That this was contingent upon moments of state regulation should make us more aware of the continuities between Fordism and so-called post-Fordism. The problem, indeed, lies with the rigidity implied by the dichotomy. Capitalism since 1945 has been not only about the standardised production of goods and services for mass markets, otherwise a particular social and economic system would have to be defined in terms of its manufacturing strategies alone. The structure of class relations in a capitalist society may be changing, but this does not mean that class antagonism had disappeared, rather that it is being restructured. In this sense, it is clear that new manufacturing and management strategies do not signal the end of social conflict, for social antagonism is not the preserve of Fordism any more than it is of any other period of capitalist development. As Costello *et al.* (1989, p. 30) argue:

> The Post-Fordists have, in their enthusiasm, plainly over-egged the pudding. They are right to emphasise the need to understand the direction of change, and to warn against ostrich-like behaviour. . . . But they have picked on some real trends and generalised them out of all recognition, with the result that their 'map' is of little use as a guide . . . for the 1990s.

For us, the uniqueness of the 'Nissan Way' lies in its combination of external political control and careful regulation of internal conflict, institutionalised in the company's image. As part of this new regime of subordination, the 'Nissan Way' rests upon control through quality, exploitation via flexibility, and surveillance via teamworking. The consensus upon which these depend and which they construct displaces social antagonism. It is because there is a process of incorporation through subordination (described in Chapters 3 and 4) that Nissan has become the first auto producer in Europe to build up company consensus through identifying workers as good company men and women first and foremost. The experience of isolation through personal exclusion and dislocation creates a dependence on the 'Nissan Way'. This allows for commitment to personal security through working for devolved worker-managing strategies (*kaizen*, VES and Neighbour Check). If this does not always work, passivity can be guaranteed as individuals are told to 'put up or shut up', as some of our respondents made clear. A family, a mortgage and 'debt in the car park' (as our interviewee John observed) do not make unemployment a realistic option.

References

Allen, J. and Massey, D. (1988) *The Economy in Question*. Beverly Hills, CA: Sage.

Altshuler, A.A. *et al.* (1984) *The Future of the Automobile*. Cambridge, MA: MIT Press.

Amin, A. and Smith, I. (1990) The British car components industry: leaner and fitter? In: Stewart *et al.*, op. cit., pp. 120–152.

Amin, A. and Tomaney, J. (forthcoming) Illusions of prosperity. In: Fasenfast, P. and Meyer, P. (eds.) *The Politics of Local Economic Policy Formation*. Basingstoke: Macmillan.

Armstrong, P., Glynn, A. and Harrison, J. (1984) *Capitalism since World War Two: the Making and Breakup of the Great Boom*. London: Fontana.

Balchin, P.N. (1990) *Regional Policy*. London: Harper & Row.

Beynon, H. (1984) *Working for Ford*. Harmondsworth: Penguin.

Beynon, H., Hudson, R. and Sadler, D. (1986) Nationalised industries and the destruction of communities: some evidence from the North East of England. *Capital and Class*, no. 29, pp. 27–57.

Braverman, H. (1974) *Labour and Monopoly Capital*. London: Monthly Review Press.

Burawoy, M. (1979) *Manufacturing Consent: Changes in the Labour Process under Monopoly Capitalism*. Chicago: University of Chicago Press.

Burawoy, M. (1985) *The Politics of Production: Factory Regimes under Capitalism and Socialism*. London: Verso.

Byrne, D. (1988) *Beyond the Inner City*. Milton Keynes: Open University Press.

Byrne, D. (1990) The end of positive planning. In: Stewart *et al.*, op. cit., pp. 151–164.

CAITS (Centre for Alternative Industrial and Technological Systems) (1986) *Flexibility: Who Needs It?* London: North London Polytechnic.

CAITS (1988) Japan comes to Vauxhall. North London Polytechnic mimeograph.

Cecchini, P. (1988) *1992 The European Challenge: The Benefits of a Single Market.* Aldershot: Wildwood House.

Chandler, J.A. and Lawless, P. (1985) *Local Authorities and the Creation of Employment.* Aldershot: Gower.

Clarke, S. (1988) Overaccumulation, class struggle and the regulation approach. *Capital and Class*, no. 36, pp. 59–92.

Clarke, S. (1991) What in the f--'s name is Fordism?. In: Gilbert, N. and Burrows, S. (eds) *Fordism and Flexibility: Divisions and Change.* Basingstoke: Macmillan.

Cochrane, A. (ed.) (1989) *Developing Local Economic Strategies.* Milton Keynes: Open University Press.

Cockburn, C. (1983) *Brothers: Male Dominance and Technological Change.* London: Pluto Press.

Cooke, P. (ed.) (1989) *Localities: The Changing Face of Urban Britain.* London: Unwin Hyman.

Costello, N., Michie, J. and Milne, S. (1989) *Beyond the Casino Economy: Planning for the 1990s.* London: Verso.

Crowther, S. and Garrahan, P. (1988) Corporate power and the local economy. *Industrial Relations Journal*, **19**(1), 51–59.

Cusamano, M.A. (1985) *The Japanese Automobile Industry: Technology and Management at Nissan and Toyota.* Cambridge, MA: Harvard University Press.

Cutler, T., Haslam, C., Williams, J. and Williams, K. (1989) *1992—The Struggle for Europe: A Critical Evaluation of the EC.* Oxford: Berg.

Dicken, P. (1983) Japanese manufacturing investment in the UK. *Area*, **15**(4), 273–284.

Dicken, P. (1986) *Global Shift: Industrial Change in a Turbulent World.* London: Harper & Row.

Dohse, K., Jurgens, U. and Malsch, T. (1985) From Fordism to Toyotism. *Politics and Society*, **14**(2), 115–146.

Doray, B. (1988) *From Taylorism to Fordism: A Rational Madness.* London: Free Association Books.

Edwards, R. (1979) *Contested Terrain: The Transformation of the Workplace in the Twentieth Century.* London: Basic Books.

Elger, T. (1989) Change and continuity in the Labour process: technical innovation and work reorganisation in the 1980's. Paper presented to the Work, Employment and Society Conference, University of Durham, September 1989.

European Commission (1989) *Panorama of EC Industry 1989*, chapter 14. Luxembourg: Commission of the European Communities.

Fairbrother, P. and Waddington, J. (1990) The politics of trade unionism: evidence, policy and theory. *Capital and Class*, no. 41, pp. 15–56.

Foster, J. and Wolfson, C. (1989) Corporate reconstruction and business union-ism: the lessons of Caterpillar and Ford. *New Left Review*, no. 174, pp. 51-66.

Friedman, A.L. (1977) *Industry and Labour: Class Struggle at Work and Monopoly Capitalism*. London: Macmillan.

Garrahan, P. (1986) Nissan in the North East. *Capital and Class*, no. 27, pp. 5-13.

Garrahan, P. and Stewart, P. (1989) Post-Fordism, Japanisation, and the local economy. In: Proceedings of the Conference of Socialist Economists, Sheffield Polytechnic, July.

Garrahan, P. and Stewart, P. (1990) Auto unions: Sayonara? *International Labour Reports*, no. 38, pp. 22-23.

Garrahan, P. and Stewart, P. (1991a) Nothing new about Nissan? In: Law, C. (ed.) *Restructuring the Automobile Industry*. London: Routledge.

Garrahan, P. and Stewart, P. (1991b) Management control and a new regime of subordination. In: Gilbert, N. and Burrows, S. (eds) *Fordism and Flexibility: Divisions and Change*. London: Macmillan.

Garrahan, P. and Stewart, P. (1992) Working for Nissan. *Science as Culture*, forthcoming.

Gertler, M.S. (1988) The limits to flexibility: comments on the post-Fordist vision of production and its geography. *Transactions of the Institute of British Geographers*, N.S. 13, pp. 419-432.

Graham, I. (1988) Japanisation as mythology. *Industrial Relations Journal*, **19**(1), 69-75.

Gramsci, A. (1971) Americanism and Fordism. In: *Prison Notebooks*. London: Lawrence & Wishart.

Hall, B. and Wilson, P. (1989) *The North of England: Prepared for 1992?* Socialist Group of the European Parliament.

Hasluck, C. (1987) *Urban Employment: Local Labour Markets and Employment Initia-tives*. Harlow: Longman.

Hill, R.C. (1984) Transnational capitalism and urban crisis: the case of the auto industry in Detroit. In: Szeleyni, I. (ed.) *Cities in Recession*, pp. 141-159.

Hill, R.C. (1987) Global factory and company town: the changing division of labour in the international automobile industry. In: Henderson, J. and Castells, M. (eds) *Global Restructuring and Territorial Development*. London: Sage.

Hill, R.C. (1989) Comparing transnational production systems. *International Journal of Urban and Regional Research*, **13**, 462-479.

Hill, R.C. Indergaard, M. and Fujita, K. (1989) Flat Rock, home of Mazda: the social impact of a Japanese company on an American community. In: Arnesen, P.J. (ed.) *The Auto Industry Ahead: Who's Driving?* Center for Japanese Studies, University of Michigan, Ann Arbor.

Hill, S. (1988) *The Tragedy of Technology: Human Liberation Versus Domination in the Late Twentieth Century*. London: Pluto Press.

Hudson, R. (1989) *Wrecking a Region: State Policies, Party Politics, and Regional Change in the North East of England*. London: Pion.

Johnson, C. (1982) *MITI and the Japanese Economic Miracle: the Growth of Industrial policy, 1925–72*. Stanford, CA: Stanford University Press.

Junkerman, J. (1987) Nissan Tennessee. *The Progressive*, June, pp. 16–20.

King, D. (1987) *The New Right: Politics, Markets, and Citizenship*. London: Macmillan.

Knights, D. and Willmott, H. (1989) Power and subjectivity at work: from degradation to subjugation in social relations. *Sociology*, **23**(14), 535–558.

Lichtenstein, N. and Meyer, S. (1989) *On the Line: Essays in the History of Auto Work*. Champaign: University of Illinois Press.

Liepitz, A. (1986) *Miracles and Mirages*. London: Verso.

Littler, C.R. (1982) *The Development of the Labour Process in Capitalist Societies*. London: Heinemann Educational Books.

Lovering, J. (1990) Fordism's unknown successor: a comment on Scott's theory of flexible accumulation and the re-emergence of regional economies. *International Journal of Urban and Regional Research*, **14**, 159–174.

Ludvigsen Associates (1988) *The EC92 Automobile Sector*. Report to the Commission of the European Communities.

MacInnes, J. (1987) *Thatcherism at Work*. Milton Keynes: Open University Press.

Maguire, M. (1988) Work, locality and social control. *Work, Employment and Society*, **2**(1), 71–87.

Mair, A., Florida, R. and Kenney, M. (1988) The new geography of automobile production: Japanese transplants in North America. *Economic Geography*, **64**(4), 352–373.

Marquez, G. (1978) *One Hundred Years of Solitude*. Harmondsworth: Penguin.

Massey, D. (1984) *Spatial Divisions of Labour*. Basingstoke: Macmillan.

Massey, D. and Allen, J. (eds) (1988) *Uneven Re-development: Cities and Regions in Transition*. Hodder & Stoughton.

Meyer, S. (1981) *The Five Dollar Day: Labour Management and Social Control in the Ford Motor Company 1908–1921*. Albany: State University of New York Press.

Morgan, K. and Sayer, A. (1988) A modern industry in a mature region: the remaking of management labour relations. In: Massey, D. and Allen, J. (eds) op. cit., pp. 167–187.

Morris, J. (1987) Industrial restructuring, foreign direct investment, and uneven development: the case of Wales. *Environment and Planning A*, **19**, 205–224.

Murray, R. (1988) Life after Henry (Ford). *Marxism Today*, October.

NCC (1990) Cars: the cost of trade restrictions to customers. *International Trade and the Consumer, Working Paper no. 4*. National Consumer Council.

NDC (1990a) *International Investment in the North of England*. Newcastle upon Tyne: Northern Development Company.

NDC (1990b) *Japanese Investment in the North of England*. Northern Development Company, Newcastle.

Nissan (1987) *Workshop Management*.

NMUK (Nissan Motor Manufacturing (UK) Ltd) (1985) *Agreement on Terms and*

Conditions of Employment between Nissan Motor Manufacturing (UK) Ltd and Amalgamated Engineering Union.

NMUK (Nissan Motor Manufacturing (UK) Ltd) (1988, 1990), *Information Pack.*

NRCA (1987) *The State of the Northern Region, 1986.* Newcastle upon Tyne: Northern Region Councils Association.

Oakland, J.S. (1989) *Total Quality Management.* Oxford: Heinemann.

Okayama, R. (1986) Industrial relations in the Japanese automobile industry 1945–70: the case of Toyota. In: Tolliday, S. and Zeitlin, J. (eds) *The Automobile Industry and Its Workers.* Cambridge: Polity Press, pp. 168–189.

Oliver, N. and Wilkinson, B. (1988) *The Japanisation of British Industry.* Oxford: Blackwell.

Overbeek, H. (1990) *Global Capitalism and National Decline: The Thatcher Decade in Perspective.* London: Unwin Hyman.

Palmer, J. (1988) *Trading Places.* London: Radius.

Parker, M. (1985) *Inside the Circle: A Union Guide to QWL.* A Labor Notes Book. Boston, MA: South End Press.

Parker, M. and Slaughter, J. (1988) *Choosing Sides: Unions and the Team Concept.* A Labor Notes Book. Boston, MA: South End Press.

Parker, M. and Slaughter, J. (1989) Dealing with good management. *Labour Research Review*, 8(2) (Fall).

Piore, M.J. and Sabel, C. (1984) *The Second Industrial Divide.* London: Basic Books.

Pollert, A. (1988a) Dismantling flexibility. *Capital and Class*, no. 34, pp. 42–75.

Pollert, A. (1988b) The 'Flexible Firm': fixation or fact? *Work, Employment and Society*, 2(3) 281–316.

Reid, N. (1989) Spatial patterns of Japanese investment in the US automobile industry. *Industrial Relations Journal*, 13, 49–59.

Robinson, F. (1990) *The Great North?* Report from the Centre for Urban and Regional Development Studies, University of Newcastle upon Tyne.

Robinson, F., Wren, C. and Goddard, J. (1987) *Economic Development Policies.* Oxford: Clarendon Press.

Rubenstein, J. (1987) Further changes in the American automobile industry. *Geographical Review*, 77, 359–362.

Rubenstein, J. (1988) Changing distribution of American motor vehicle parts suppliers. *Geographical Review*, 78, 288–298.

Saga, I. (no date) Labour relations in Japan: the case of the Nissan Motor Company. Mimeograph, University of Tokyo.

Saga, I. (1983) The development of new technology in Japan: mainly its effect on work. Bulletin no. 5 of the Socialist Research Centre, Hosei University.

Sayer, A. (1986) New developments in manufacturing: the Just-In-Time system. *Capital and Class*, no. 30, pp. 43–72.

Sayer, A. (1989) Postfordism in question. *International Journal of Urban and Regional Research*, 13(4), 666–693.

Schoenberger, E. (1987) Technical and organisational change in automobile production: spatial implications. *Regional Studies*, 21(3), 199–214.

Sheard, P. (1983) Auto production systems in Japan: organisational and locational features. *Australian Geographical Studies*, **21**, 49–68.

Slaughter, J. (1987) The team concept in the US auto industry: implications for unions. *Labor Notes*.

Stewart, P., Garrahan, P. and Crowther, S. (eds) (1990) *Restructuring for Economic Flexibility*. Aldershot: Avebury.

Stone, I. (1988) Shipbuilding on Wearside: reviewing the prospects. Mimeograph, Department of Economics, Newcastle upon Tyne Polytechnic.

Stone, I. and Stevens, J. (1986) Economic restructuring and employment change on Wearside since 1971. Sunderland Polytechnic External Development Unit Report for the European Community/Borough of Sunderland.

Stone, I. and Stevens, J. (1988) Employment on Wearside: trends and prospects. *Northern Economic Review*, no. 12, Winter.

Thompson, P. (1983) *The Nature of Work*. Basingstoke: Macmillan.

Thompson, P. and Bannon, E. (1985) *Working the System: The Shop Floor and New Technology*. London: Pluto Press.

Tolliday, S. and Zeitlin, J. (eds) (1986) *The Auto Industry and Its Workers*. Cambridge: Polity Press.

Tomaney, J. (1990) The reality of workplace flexibility. *Capital and Class*, no. 40, pp. 29–60.

Totsuka, H. (1982) Japanese trade union attitudes towards rationalisation. Mimeograph, paper presented to the International Political Science Association XIIth World Congress.

TUSIU (1989) *Labour and Economy*. Trade Union Studies Information Unit, Newcastle upon Tyne.

Wainwright, H. and Elliot, D. (1982) *The Lucas Plan: A New Trade Unionism in the Making*. London: Allison & Busby.

Westwood, S. (1984) *All Day, Every Day: Factory and Family in the Making of Women's Lives*. London: Pluto Press.

Wickens, P. (1987) *The Road to Nissan*. London: Macmillan.

Williams, K., Cutler, T., Williams, J. and Haslam, C. (1987a) The end of mass production. In: Thompson, G. (ed.) *Industrial Policy: UK and US debates*. Routledge, pp. 163–196.

Williams, K., Cutler, T., Williams, J. and Haslam, C. (1987b) *The Breakdown of Austin Rover*. Oxford: Berg.

Williamson, H. (1989) Back in the melting pot? Rethinking trade union perspectives on Japanese motor industry investment in Britain and 'Japanese-style' industrial relations. Mimeograph, Centre for Alternative Industrial and Technological Systems, London.

Womack, J., Roos, D. and Jones, D. (1990) *The Machine That Changed the World*. Rawson Associates.

Yamamoto, K. (1980) Labour–management relations at Nissan Motor Co. Ltd. *Annals of the Institute of Social Science*, no. 21, University of Tokyo.

Index